A GIFT FOR

FROM

DATE

LET IN THE
light

50 Devotions
to Confidently Know God Is
Good and Guiding Your Steps

The Proverbs 31 Ministries Team

WITH A FOREWORD BY

Lysa TerKeurst

THOMAS NELSON
Since 1798

LET IN THE LIGHT

© 2025 Proverbs 31 Ministries

All rights reserved. No portion of this book may be reproduced, stored in a retrieval system, or transmitted in any form or by any means—electronic, mechanical, photocopy, recording, scanning, or other—except for brief quotations in critical reviews or articles, without the prior written permission of the publisher.

Published in Nashville, Tennessee, by Thomas Nelson. Thomas Nelson is a registered trademark of HarperCollins Christian Publishing, Inc.

Thomas Nelson titles may be purchased in bulk for educational, business, fundraising, or sales promotional use. For information, please email SpecialMarkets@ThomasNelson.com.

Unless otherwise noted, Scripture quotations are from the Christian Standard Bible®. Copyright © 2017 by Holman Bible Publishers. Used by permission. Christian Standard Bible® and CSB® are federally registered trademarks of Holman Bible Publishers.

Scripture quotations marked ESV are from the ESV® Bible (The Holy Bible, English Standard Version®). Copyright © 2001 by Crossway, a publishing ministry of Good News Publishers. All rights reserved.

Scripture quotations marked NIV are from the Holy Bible, New International Version®, NIV®. Copyright © 1973, 1978, 1984, 2011 by Biblica, Inc.® Used by permission of Zondervan. All rights reserved worldwide. www.zondervan.com. The "NIV" and "New International Version" are trademarks registered in the United States Patent and Trademark Office by Biblica, Inc.®

Any internet addresses, phone numbers, or company or product information printed in this book are offered as a resource and are not intended in any way to be or to imply an endorsement by Thomas Nelson, nor does Thomas Nelson vouch for the existence, content, or services of these sites, phone numbers, companies, or products beyond the life of this book.

Cover design: Gabriella Wikidal

Interior design: Jeff Jansen

Photography by Natalya Vdovina/Shutterstock (p. vi); Azaliya (Elya Vatel)/Adobe Stock (p. x); Vera Kuttelvaserova/Adobe Stock (p. xiii); Franta Krivan/Adobe Stock (p. xiv); shine.graphics/Shutterstock (p. 4); Matthew Troke/Shutterstock (p. 8); KichiginShutterstock (p. 12); Yavdat/Shutterstock (p. 17); AtlasStudio/Shutterstock (p. 21); Poramet/Adobe Stock (p. 22); Laurentiu/Shutterstock (p. 30); narongchaihlaw/Adobe Stock (p. 33); nadiya_sergey/Shutterstock (p. 44); CAPIXEL/Shutterstock (p. 49); LutsenkoLarissa/Shutterstock (p. 62); apimook/Adobe Stock (p. 79); Eugen Hoppe/Wirestock/Adobe Stock (p. 80); KoralFox/Adobe Stock (p. 95); Nataliaova/Shutterstock (p. 97); Sosnina Olga/Shutterstock (p. 98); Alex Stemmer/Shutterstock (p. 110); habibalm124/Shutterstock (p. 114); Buntovskikh Olga/Shutterstock (p. 117); Manzooranmai/Shutterstock (p. 119); pop_thailand/Adobe Stock (p. 120); Konstiantyn/Adobe Stock (p. 126); Galyna Andrushko/Adobe Stock (p. 129); Floral Deco/Adobe Stock (p. 140); aleksandarfilip/Adobe Stock (p. 147); AnnGaysorn/Shutterstock (p. 149); Tanaly/Adobe Stock (p. 153); Artem Popov/Adobe Stock (p. 155); Anna_ok/Adobe Stock (p. 157); LedyX/Shutterstock (p. 158); yotrakbutda/Adobe Stock (p. 168); irenastar/Adobe Stock (p. 171); Igisheva Maria/Shutterstock (p. 176); Viktoriia Lomtieva/Shutterstock (p. 183); Viktoriia/Adobe Stock (p. 184); and gamjai/Adobe Stock (p. 193).

ISBN 978-1-4002-5374-6 (HC)

ISBN 978-1-4002-5376-0 (audiobook)

ISBN 978-1-4002-5375-3 (eBook)

Printed in India

25 26 27 28 29 MAN 10 9 8 7 6 5 4 3 2 1

To the staff at Proverbs 31 Ministries: Thank you for faithfully bringing your gifts and talents to share the Word of God with the world. Together we are taking steps to eradicate biblical poverty.

To the writers of this devotional: Thank you for saying yes to this project and shining your light for the world, bringing glory to God with your writing.

> May the Lord bless you and protect you;
> may the Lord make his face shine on you
> and be gracious to you;
> may the Lord look with favor on you
> and give you peace. (Numbers 6:24–26)

Contents

    A Letter from Lysa TerKeurst xi

Part 1: God Is Light 1

    1: **Light Has Dawned,** Sarah Freymuth 2
    2: **The Father of Lights,** Carole Holiday 6
    3: **Our God, the Everlasting Light,** Rachel Marie Kang 10
    4: **The Lord Is My Light,** Hadassah Treu 14
    5: **Keep the Lights On, Lord,** Rachel Booth Smith 18

Part 2: God Reveals Himself in Light 23

    6: **God's Name in Lights,** Dr. Joel Muddamalle 24
    7: **To Light the Way,** Sarah Freymuth 27
    8: **God's Presence and Glory in Our Midst,** Wendy Blight . . . 31
    9: **The Reflected Radiance of God,** Stacy J. Lowe 35
    10: **When We're Standing on Holy Ground,** Carole Holiday . . . 38
    11: **God Shines a Flashlight to Guide Our Souls,**
        Dorina Lazo Gilmore-Young 41

Part 3: We Have Walked in Darkness 45

    12: **Walk in the Light as He Is in the Light,** Dr. Avril Occilien-Similien . . . 46
    13: **A Wing and a Prayer,** Claire Foxx 50
    14: **The Lasting Light in Our Lamps,** June Chapman 53
    15: **Our God of (Im)Possible,** Meghan Mellinger 56
    16: **The Silent Rhythm of Life,** Dr. Alicia Britt Chole 59

Part 4: God's Blessings Shine ... 63

17: **Whose Light Is It Anyway?**, Claire Foxx. ... 64
18: **Just Enough Light for the Next Step**, Meghan Mellinger ... 67
19: **God Is Still Good**, Hadassah Treu ... 70
20: **The Brightly Lit Path**, Carole Holiday ... 73
21: **We Bless Him When We Feel Blessed and Even When We Don't**,
Rachel Marie Kang ... 76

Part 5: Darkness Will Not Last Forever ... 81

22: **Stepping Out of the Shadows**, Sarah Freymuth ... 82
23: **Will Morning Ever Come?**, Alicia Bruxvoort ... 85
24: **When You Feel Lost, Jesus Is the Way**, Ashley Morgan Jackson ... 88
25: **The Same God Will Deliver You**, Meredith Houston Carr ... 91
26: **We Are Chosen to Shine Light in the Darkness**,
Dorina Lazo Gilmore-Young ... 94

Part 6: A New Dawn Is Coming ... 99

27: **The Treasure of Night Faith**, Dr. Alicia Britt Chole ... 100
28: **No Longer Afraid of the Dark**, Meredith Houston Carr ... 103
29: **Hope in the Darkness**, Stacy J. Lowe ... 106
30: **I See Your Father in You**, Elizabeth Laing Thompson ... 109
31: **The Breathtaking Glory of Jesus' Light for All**, Asheritah Ciuciu ... 113
32: **Shadows Prove the Light**, Eric Gagnon ... 116

Part 7: Jesus Is the Light of the World ... 121

33: **Message of the Magi**, Meghan Mellinger ... 122
34: **A Spectacular Light for Everyone**, Dorina Lazo Gilmore-Young ... 125
35: **Dawn of Grace**, Brenda Bradford Ottinger ... 128

36: **Stick Close to the Light,** Alicia Bruxvoort. 131
37: **The Quickest Way to Overcome the Darkness,** Laura Lacey Johnson . . 134
38: **We Have Seen His Glory,** Alicia Bruxvoort. 137

Part 8: Children of Light, Called to Shine 141

39: **Shine Pretty Shine,** Meghan Mellinger. 142
40: **The Antidote to Identity Theft,** Meredith Houston Carr. 145
41: **Prepared for the Storm,** Ashley Morgan Jackson 148
42: **The Light of Life Lives in You,** June Chapman 151
43: **Living Lanterns,** Brenda Bradford Ottinger 154

Part 9: Darkness Is Defeated 159

44: **A New Day Is Dawning,** Sarah Freymuth 160
45: **The Light of Christ Will Lead Us Home,** Rachel Marie Kang. 163
46: **Living in Anticipation,** Carrie Zeilstra 166
47: **Finding Purpose in the Pause,** Ashley Morgan Jackson 170
48: **Worshiping the Most High King over Every Lesser Thing,**
    June Chapman 173
49: **Our New "Irreversible,"** Hadassah Treu 177
50: **From Solar-Powered to God-Powered,** Carrie Zeilstra 180

About the Writers 185

Hi friend,

Here's what I've come to know: One of Satan's greatest desires is to separate us from God. And he attempts to accomplish this by separating us from God's Word.

Satan wants us to see the Bible as a burden instead of as the blessing it really is. He will try to make us think we don't have enough time to read God's Word. Or that we're not smart enough to study and understand it. He'll also suggest the lie that it's too hard to live out the truths in God's Word.

The minute any of these thoughts pop into our minds, we must recognize them as messages of the Enemy trying to lure us into a trap. Of course he wants to separate us from God's Word: *It's our trusted handbook for living.*

Psalm 119:105 says, "Your word is *a lamp* for my feet and *a light* on my path" (italics added). And then just a few verses later, we read, "The revelation of your words brings *light* and gives *understanding* to the inexperienced" (v. 130, italics added).

These verses hold such a dear place in my heart. I personally know it's possible to encounter the power of God's light even in dark and difficult seasons.

Friend, make no mistake—we are in a battle. A daily one. Darkness is trying with all its might to overcome, *but light always wins*. Even in nature, no matter how hard the darkness tries to shut it out, light always breaks through.

Knowing this truth, our hearts can hope!

Are you ready to refuse the Enemy's temptation to dwell in doubt and defeat?

Does your weary and discouraged heart long to feel excitement around God's Word again?

Is there an area of your life that needs a touch of God's light? Mine too.

Now . . . let's let in the light together.

Many blessings,

Lysa

Lysa TerKeurst
President and Chief Visionary Officer,
Proverbs 31 Ministries

PART 1

God Is Light

Light is symbolic of purity, truth, beauty, and life. When the Bible says, "God is light," we understand it to mean that God is the source of everything good and glorious. There is no darkness or even a shadow within Him.

1

Light Has Dawned

SARAH FREYMUTH

This is the message we have heard from him and declare to you: God is light, and there is absolutely no darkness in him.

1 JOHN 1:5

Winter keeps coming, which feels like a heaviness in the air and in my chest if I admit it. Sometimes it's hard to see my way through this time of perpetual darkness with the appearance of the sun so late and its sinking so early in the day. It's hard to keep waking up at my normal alarm time when I'm burrowed under comfy covers and the world outside looks like it's still the middle of the night.

On the shortest day of the year, the winter solstice, we see the least amount of light. A veil of darkness makes many of us wish we could curl up and hibernate all winter.

Like the literal dark of this winter day, emotional or spiritual exhaustion can overtake us with the hard things we endure. Whether it's more devastation on the news, late nights worrying about a prodigal, another month barely paying the bills, or a season where joy has been elusive, we're faced with that same temptation to close our eyes to all of it and hope when we open them that things will be different.

It's hard to keep slogging through when life is difficult and darkness prevails. Will this winter of our hearts always last?

We sit and wait and wonder.

Then we see it. Peeling back the dark . . . light has dawned.

The Bright and Morning Star arises, alight with life and hope. Jesus has come into this world and taken darkness captive; He has overshadowed it by the power of His light. In Him there is no darkness, and He does not fear going to the depths for us. The darkness is not dark to Him. Nothing in your situation can scare Him away; it's the opposite. When you call out to Him in your suffering, He draws close.

Jesus came to a world riddled with darkness, destruction, temptation, and brokenness. He came headfirst and lived among us, calling all to Him, the Light of life. When we are weary, He is our strength. When we run out of steam, He keeps us going. When we face the lies of the Evil One, He battles for us, reminding us of our worth in Him.

He is the light that cannot be overcome. This is the hope we hold close, the joy that illuminates our hearts because we can shift our focus from the weak winter sun to the eternal Son who sets us free to live in His light and shine it out to others.

Mindful of this truth, waking up today doesn't seem as harsh as usual. Layers of blue and gray and white clouds climb the sky, patterned in winter's blanket, a layered beauty I know the sun resides behind.

Glory, the Light of the World has come.

JOURNAL PROMPT

How is Jesus comforting you with His light and love in this season?

_____

_____

_____

_____

_____

_____

_____

Reframe your thinking on something you're struggling with. How does the light of Jesus' power and love change how you approach it?

_____

_____

_____

_____

_____

_____

_____

_____

2

The Father of Lights

CAROLE HOLIDAY

*Every good and perfect gift is from above,
coming down from the Father of lights,
who does not change like shifting shadows.*

JAMES 1:17

I loved Nancy Drew mystery books when I was a kid. The classic characters captivated my ten-year-old imagination. Predictably, the villain appeared hanging in the shadows and was portrayed in terms that told the reader this ne'er-do-well was shifty, reliably unreliable, sometimes there and sometimes not—always one who could not be trusted.

When I read James's descriptive words, "shifting shadows," I thought back to those literary villains who hid in the darkness.

Writing to the scattered believers who were enduring trials, James reminded us that our God is not one who lurks in the shadows. God is nothing like that.

In fact, James explained that there is no shadow in Him at all. No villainous shiftiness can be contained in the One James called the Father of lights.

What was James referring to with this name? Is it a prompt, perhaps, to meditate in awe on the One who hung the glowing celestial orbs in the sky, the heavenly parent who perfectly planted the stars, willing the planets to turn with unmatched precision? If He could do all that, is it any wonder that God could speak light into existence? And if God created light, He remains the eternal source of that light. The *Father* of lights.

Picture the sun, our solar system's only star, suspended center stage in the heavens. Its nature makes it impossible to contain darkness. It is constant, ever-present, and created by the One who shares the same qualities.

Our heavenly Father doesn't have a dark side. All sides of God are light. Because of that, there is no side we cannot see, no fickleness that leaves us wondering if God's character will shift and surprise us with unknown parts of Him. As a result, the only gifts that can emanate from Him are consistent with His goodness. Dark cannot be born of light.

James wanted to remind the suffering saints that God was not the author of their misery. Their trials were not concocted by Him. And, hurting reader, the trials you are experiencing were not placed in your path by a shady side of God that wishes to trick you. Sometimes we need to remind ourselves of God's goodness.

That's why James stated the case plainly: "Every good and perfect gift is from above" (James 1:17). He wanted to settle that debate once and for all.

Many times I have sung the words of one of the most endearing hymns that speak to this faithful aspect of God. Thomas Chisholm's "Great Is Thy Faithfulness" never fails to trigger goose bumps as the lyric "There is no shadow of turning with Thee" reassures me that God remains immovable, delivering gifts from the very core of His being. He drives away darkness and ensures a constant, unchanging, eternal light.

JOURNAL PROMPT

How does knowing that God does not change "like shifting shadows" impact your view of your circumstances or your understanding of God?

3

Our God, the Everlasting Light

RACHEL MARIE KANG

The sun will no longer be your light by day, and the brightness of the moon will not shine on you. The LORD will be your everlasting light, and your God will be your splendor.

ISAIAH 60:19

There we were, standing on the sidewalk and staring up at the sky just like the rest of North America. We were waiting for the sky to dim, all of us waiting for the darkness—that rare moment of totality.

After hours of watching the clock, it finally happened: The moon hid the light of the sun, casting a shadow that covered an eclipse path across earth. A chill settled into the air as—in those brief minutes—darkness hushed over land and sky. It was a majestic and mysterious moment, seeing this bright and shining star obscured by a celestial body four hundred times smaller than its own.

Later that day, while watching the news and scrolling through social media, I was inundated with a sharing of ancient perspectives on past solar eclipse experiences. Today, with modern technology, a solar eclipse is viewed as a natural phenomenon that is wildly sensational and, for the most part, safe. However, at one time, many people and civilizations regarded any occurrence of a solar eclipse as fearful or fateful.

Imagine a world without light switches or telescopes. Imagine witnessing these seemingly sporadic or seasonal instances of all light going out. Imagine the stories passed down through generations, speaking of eclipses as dreaded omens, rumored harbingers of darkness and, therefore, death.

Now, with that in mind, imagine how this word from the prophet Isaiah might have been received by Zion—an ancient people well acquainted with the gravity of grief, oppression, and devastating darkness:

> The sun will no longer be your light by day, and the brightness of the moon will not shine on you. (Isaiah 60:19)

For people who looked to the sun, relying on it for everyday life and survival—heat, energy, and light—Isaiah's prediction could have been both paradigm-shifting and awe-inspiring.

Regardless of the state of Zion's surroundings, Isaiah's prophecy was astonishingly true . . . and coming true: The truth that the Lord is—and forever will be—the everlasting light. He is the one who shines before and beyond time, beyond all celestial bodies that bring the providence and promise of light.

Zion had this promise to cling to: "The LORD will be your everlasting light." Not a light that expires or can be expended but *the* everlasting light. No matter

their surroundings—in and through the seasons as manifested in nature, as well as those seasons of the soul experienced internally within their hearts—God would outlast and outshine it all.

His splendor is unequaled, never to be eclipsed by sin or sorrow or even death—*yes*, death—for in Jesus is a dawn, light and life coming from and through Him. All praise to God for the brightness He is and the brightness He brings.

And what grace that the same is true for us today. Our glorious God will and does outlast and outshine all.

JOURNAL PROMPT

In what areas of your life do you need God's light to brighten that which is dark, dreaded, or dead?

_____

_____

_____

_____

_____

_____

_____

_____

_____

_____

4
The Lord Is My Light

HADASSAH TREU

The LORD is my light and my salvation—whom should I fear?
The LORD is the stronghold of my life—whom should I dread?
PSALM 27:1

We all have fears. Research shows that most people fear losing their health, wealth, and loved ones. Some of us are afraid of heights or spiders. What worst-case scenario sends shudders along your spine in the night and makes your hands sweat?

I have struggled with a lot of fears and anxieties in my life that escalated to severe panic attacks in my forties when I desperately wanted to become a mother but couldn't. Panic attacks ushered in a complete loss of control over my reactions. The fear of death, the terror of losing control, and the dread of the next panic attack were my cruel companions for several months.

In anguish, I asked the Lord for a weapon, a word of war against the terror

I faced. He gave me an arsenal; however, I will never forget the first one that became my life verse: "The LORD is my light and my salvation—whom should I fear? The LORD is the stronghold of my life—whom should I dread?" (Psalm 27:1).

The Lord is my light. Fear clouds our perceptions, blinds us, paralyzes us, and throws us into chaos and confusion. We lose orientation and can't see our way out. We are stuck. But the Lord brings light, helps us see the path ahead, and enables us to take the next step. His presence is like a blanket of peace that calms our nervous systems.

The Lord is my salvation. When chained by fear, we need God's help. Our souls can lean on Him, trusting that He will provide timely help, wisdom, healing, and everything we need to break the chains and walk in freedom. Fear is a deadly enemy, but the Lord is our mighty Savior.

The Lord is the stronghold of my life. Fear shows us how fragile we are, full of limitations and easily shaken. We need a solid foundation under our feet, an eternal rock to support and hold us when we disintegrate into a thousand pieces. The Lord remains our unlimited source of strength, support, and safety, holding us together always.

In my battle with fear and panic attacks, these three truths about God helped me stay focused on the protective presence of the Lord and prepared me to receive His help and provision. This powerful declaration of faith opened the door to my healing and growth in the only healthy fear: the fear of the Lord.

The fear of the Lord is the most powerful antidote and therapy against all other fears and worries. It sets our hearts in the right position of reverence and awe toward God as the only almighty, sovereign God, Creator, and Master of creation. It is an attitude that acknowledges Him as the only One with supreme authority over everything and everyone, over life and death.

When we put our unconditional faith in the Lord as our light, salvation, and stronghold, we experience how all other fears disperse like a mist in the sun. We can trust Him with our worst-case scenarios and the terrors of our souls.

JOURNAL PROMPT

What are your greatest fears? Using the three truths about God from Psalm 27:1, try writing your own declaration of how the Lord will help you through these fears. For example: *Because the Lord is my light, I can think clearly and make good decisions.*

_____

_____

_____

_____

_____

_____

_____

_____

_____

_____

_____

_____

_____

5

Keep the Lights On, Lord

RACHEL BOOTH SMITH

Then God said, "Let there be lights in the expanse of the sky to separate the day from the night. They will serve as signs for seasons and for days and years. They will be lights in the expanse of the sky to provide light on the earth." And it was so.

GENESIS 1:14–15

As my kids grew up, I was mesmerized by their lives. Watching how their bodies miraculously grew and their minds made brand-new connections was incredible. They were complex and beautiful, and I knew I needed supernatural insight to guide them well. The weight of my own shortcomings accompanied my wonder. How would I keep up with their curious minds and tender hearts?

I longed for them to stay far from darkness in their relationships, rooms, and souls. Even more, I hoped our home would feel secure enough to welcome vulnerability. Knowing how damaging shame and lies can be to our souls, my daily prayer as I walked through our home became five simple words: "Keep the lights on, Lord."

I knew God would answer because it's who He is. He's always had power over light.

Genesis 1:14–19 records God's creation of the sun and moon. He called the sun "the greater light" and the moon "the lesser light" (v. 16). Light is under God's command as He powerfully starts and ends the day, sets the seasons, and lights our days so we can see our way. Light radiates from the sun, but the sun's power comes from God.

The sun was also a sign of justice to the people of the ancient Near East. And God is our source of justice. Just as the day brings to light things hiding in the dark, God exposes any evil that tries to thrive in the shadows.

"And God saw that it was good" (Genesis 1:18). Light and justice are good things. Light is necessary for survival; justice protects the vulnerable and invites humanity to flourish. It takes a good God to create good things, and in creation, God declared over and over that *He* is good. We can trust Him to handle our days, light the way, and do it all with justice.

I prayed for the lights to stay on in my family and home. Slowly, God showed me that I needed that prayer for myself too. Secret sins, relationship ruptures, and false narratives loved to curl up in the dark corners of my mind. When God exposes the evil that is trying to grow, His love accompanies His light—He comes to illuminate our need for healing, not to put a brutal spotlight on our shame. His merciful conviction is part of His goodness in creation.

God kept the lights on for my children when they were little and continues to do the same for me. May we all trust the God whose light spills into our lives, inviting us to flourish and find every good thing in Him.

JOURNAL PROMPT

Do you feel like the "lights are on" in your life? Remembering that your vulnerability is safe with God, invite Him to shine His good light on any areas of your life that need flourishing, justice, or exposure. Knowing that the Holy Spirit wants only good things for you, invite Him to convict you of any sin trying to grow. Confess your sins to God and receive His forgiveness. He is gentle, He is kind, and He is for your healing.

When you are finished journaling, finish with this little prayer: "Keep the lights on, Lord."

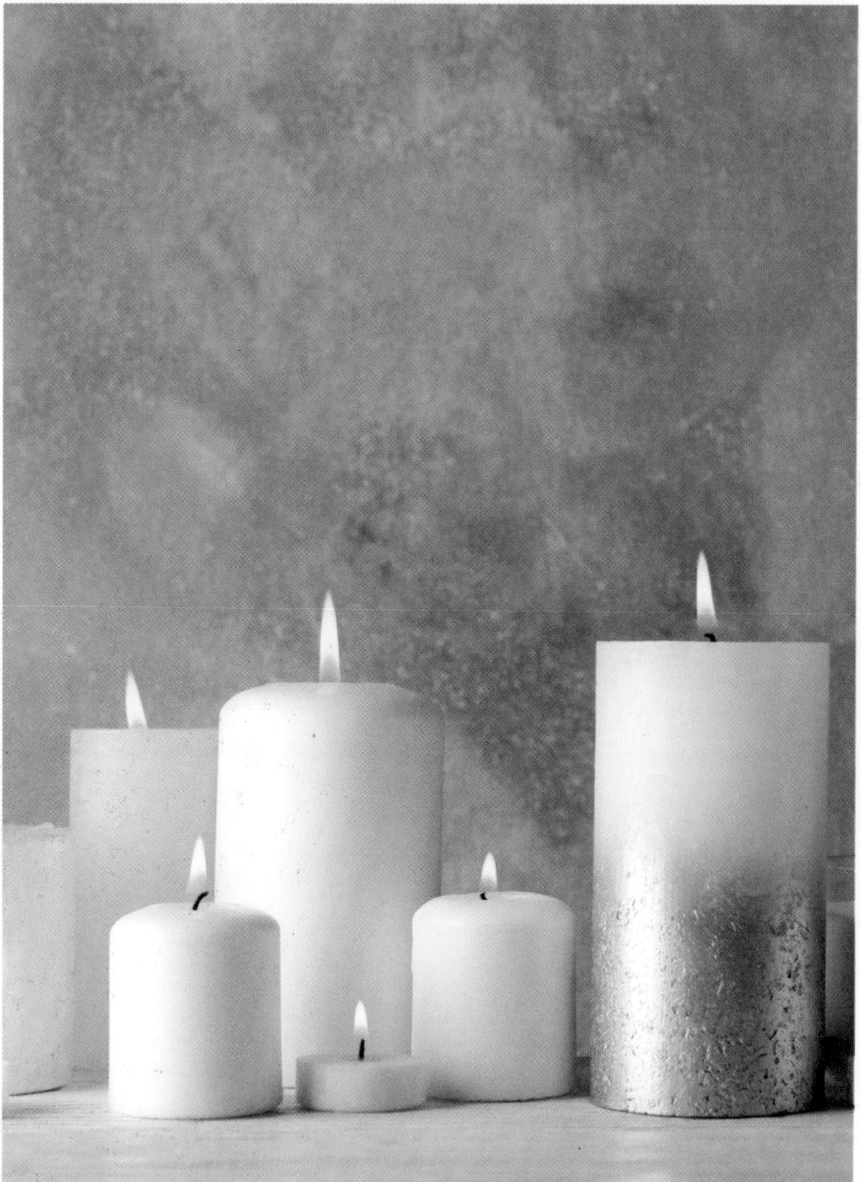

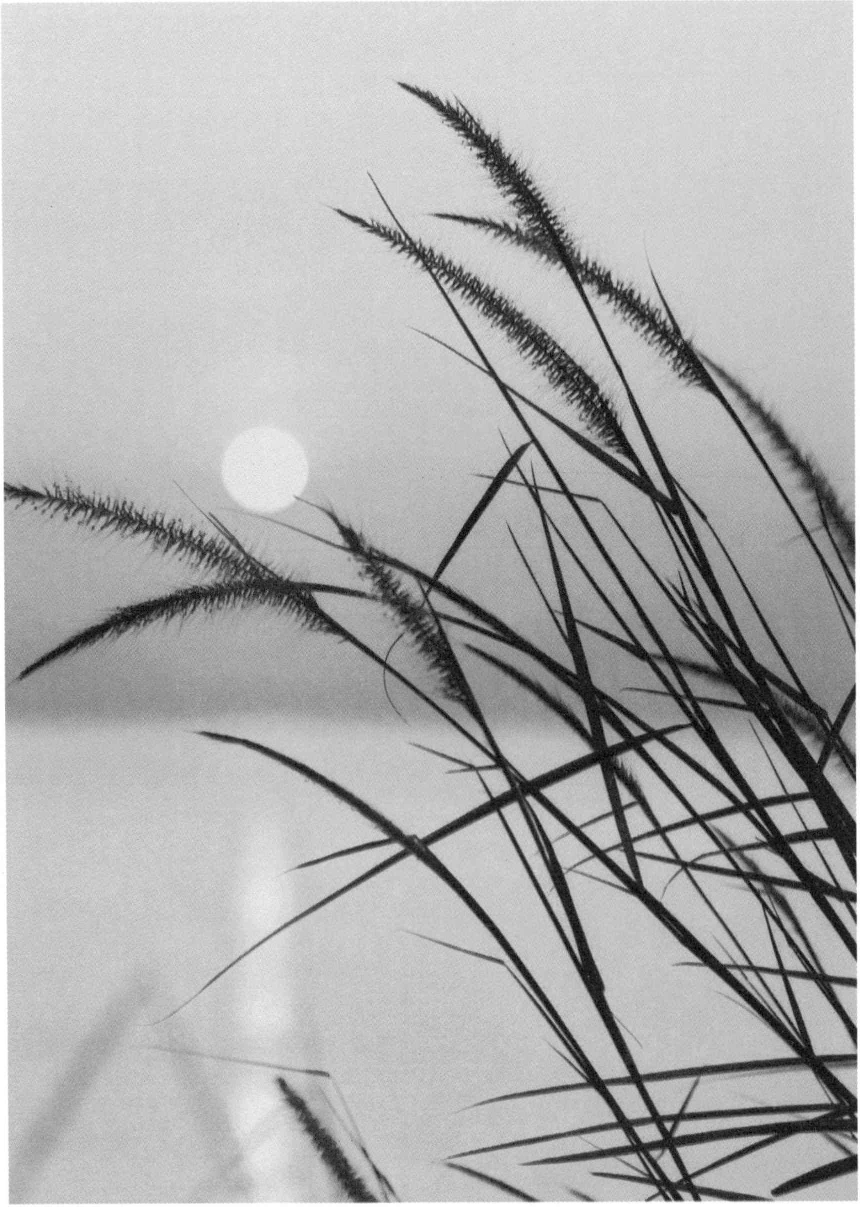

PART 2

God Reveals Himself in Light

From the first act of creation to a burning bush, to a pillar of fire, and even to the transfiguration of Jesus, God has chosen to reveal Himself to His people through light. Light captures our attention and draws us toward it . . . inviting us into God's divine presence and love.

6

God's Name in Lights

DR. JOEL MUDDAMALLE

Then the angel of the LORD appeared to him in a flame of fire within a bush. As Moses looked, he saw that the bush was on fire but was not consumed. So Moses thought, "I must go over and look at this remarkable sight. Why isn't the bush burning up?" When the LORD saw that he had gone over to look, God called out to him from the bush, "Moses, Moses!" "Here I am," he answered.

EXODUS 3:2–4

When my wife, Britt, and I were newlyweds, we kept learning new things about each other. She learned about my obsession with Chicago sports and deep-dish pizza. I learned about her passion for Hot Tamales candies and watching the same movie repeatedly. But one of the things she didn't know was the name my family called me.

Britt had known me only as Joel. But my family and childhood friends called me Joey. Britt looked at me once and said, "Okay, Joey it is." And since then, she's only ever called me Joey.

Today, if you hear someone call me "Joey," there's a good chance we have a track record of trust and a relationship that is unique and special.

In Exodus 3:2–4, we find a remarkable moment in the relationship between God and His people—the revelation of God's name through the use of light.

Exodus 3:2 starts by saying that the angel of the Lord appeared to Moses "within a bush." And then Moses saw an incredible thing: a burning bush that never burned up. When he explored further, the text explicitly says, "God called out to him from the bush." Did you catch that? The angel of the Lord was within the bush, but then God Himself called out from the bush. So which one was it? And why is this even important?

First, let's start with why it's so important. Here we find that God uses "light" as an image to reveal Himself to His people. But then, a few verses later, God discloses His intimate name to Moses—Yahweh.

This name is often referred to by Old Testament scholars as the *Tetragrammaton*, and mystery and deep reverence surround it because it's so special. When I was in seminary learning Hebrew and had to read out loud, my professor would have us use an alternate word like *Adonai* when we came across the Tetragrammaton as a reminder of how sacred the Lord is. This was also the practice of rabbinic Judaism as a precaution against taking the name of the Lord in vain. The best translation of this name is "I am who was, I am who is, and I am who will always be." Or, in other words, God is simply the great "I Am."

When God revealed His name to Moses, it was an invitation to know Him in a unique way, just as those closest to me know me as "Joey."

Second, why does it matter that the "angel of the Lord" was "within a bush"? Biblical theologians make the observation that the angel of the Lord in the Old Testament was none other than the preincarnate Christ. And in the

New Testament, Jesus referred to Himself as the great "I Am" in the Gospel of John (8:24, 28, 58; 13:19; 18:6).

In the Old Testament, God revealed Himself through fire. And simultaneously a seed was planted that was intended to anticipate the long-awaited Messiah, Jesus.

What an encouraging thought for us today. No matter how dark things get for us, light always overcomes the darkness. Light brings revelation, and there is no greater revelation than God Himself. Scripture continually reminds us that God *has always been* revealing Himself, He *is* revealing Himself, and He *will continue to* reveal Himself. As we grow in our knowledge of God, we can truly declare that He is the great "I Am."

JOURNAL PROMPT

Scripture shows us that God longs for us to know Him. How has God shown Himself to you in the past? This could be a fresh understanding of who He is, an answered prayer, or a sign that showed your prayers were heard.

_____

_____

_____

_____

_____

_____

_____

_____

7

To Light the Way

SARAH FREYMUTH

*The Lord went ahead of them in a pillar of cloud
to lead them on their way during the day
and in a pillar of fire to give them light at night,
so that they could travel day or night.*

EXODUS 13:21

Sometimes the darkness threatens to swallow me whole. Thoughts that swirl or an illness that lingers too long turn my "What if?" questions into a growing, overwhelming fear. *Can anyone see me stuck here? What is to become of my countless worries that try to keep me struggling in the dark?*

Have you also wrestled in the night without a straightforward way through? You're in good company.

When God brought the Israelites out of slavery in Egypt, He knew the temptations of their hearts to turn back when things got tough:

> When Pharaoh let the people go, God did not lead them along the road to the land of the Philistines, even though it was nearby; for God said, "The people will change their minds and return to Egypt if they face war." So he led the people around toward the Red Sea along the road of the wilderness. (Exodus 13:17–18)

God longs for intimacy with us and is interested in developing our character. He took the Israelites into a place where they would be completely dependent on Him, and along the way, they experienced something miraculous:

> The Lord went ahead of them in a pillar of cloud to lead them on their way during the day and in a pillar of fire to give them light at night, so that they could travel day or night. The pillar of cloud by day and the pillar of fire by night never left its place in front of the people. (vv. 13:21–22)

The Lord went before them in a pillar of fire, illuminating the deep dark of the wilderness as they traveled unknown lands. He did not leave them alone there; He made His presence known, and day by day and night by night, He led them.

When we don't know what to do, we can turn toward the One who does. God goes before us, lighting our paths like a pillar of fire that brings us closer to His heart, even if we don't have all the information or a situation lingers unresolved. Our comfort is closeness with the God of the Israelites, with the God of our hearts.

Look to the Lord to light the way. Do you see His miraculous presence? When you are tempted to despair, stand in the strength of the Lord and His marvelous light. He is the one you can lean on, the one who leads you forward.

JOURNAL PROMPT

Where do you need God to help you through the dark? Look for His presence with you even now, and thank Him for leading the way.

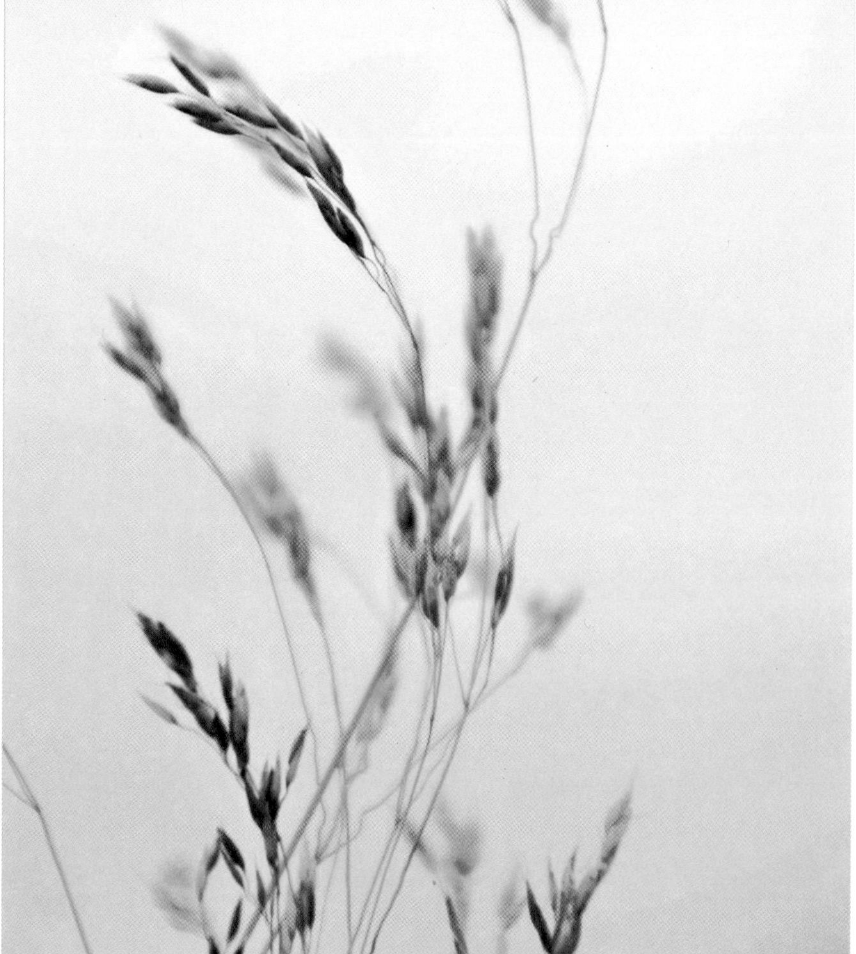

8

God's Presence and Glory in Our Midst

WENDY BLIGHT

*The appearance of the L*ORD*'s glory to the Israelites*
was like a consuming fire on the mountaintop.

EXODUS 24:17

Nervousness crept into my heart as my kids and I hopped in the car to begin our long journey from Charlotte, North Carolina, to Dallas, Texas, without my husband. As I backed down the driveway, we prayed for God to be with us, go before us, and show us glimpses of His presence and glory along the way.

Because of the long trip ahead of us, I longed to know that God's presence was near. In a way, we were like the Israelites who needed to know the same thing during their journey through the wilderness. In Exodus 24, the Israelites were six months into their journey when Moses led the elders up Mount Sinai. Upon arrival, "they saw the God of Israel. Beneath his feet was something like a pavement made of lapis lazuli, as clear as the sky itself" (v. 10).

A couple of verses later, God invited Moses alone to ascend farther up the mountain: "Come up to me on the mountain and stay there so that I may give you the stone tablets with the law and commandments I have written for their instruction" (v. 12).

Reread God's words to Moses:

Come up . . . to Me.
Stay . . . with Me.
I will give you . . . My Word.

The words we read a few verses later inspire awe and wonder: "When Moses went up the mountain, the cloud covered it. The glory of the Lord settled on Mount Sinai, and the cloud covered it for six days. On the seventh day he called to Moses from the cloud. The appearance of the Lord's glory to the Israelites was like a consuming fire on the mountaintop" (vv. 15–17).

What a sight it must have been! The *glory* of the Lord settled on the mountain, visible to all the Israelites. God revealed Himself through the light . . . His glory was like a consuming fire.

Each step of the journey, God gave Moses glimpses of His glory (the burning bush, pillars of fire and cloud). And here God invited Moses to step into His very presence and glory.

Because of Jesus, we receive this same invitation.

My child, *come meet* with Me.
Come, *stay* with Me.
I will give you My Word.

The more you and I meet with God, the more we receive from Him, the more His Spirit fills us and His glory shines through us to be His light to this dark world. Hallelujah!

As for our trip to Dallas, God answered our prayers and showed us glimpses of His presence and glory. The invisible became visible. The day brought cloudless, clear blue skies, but every few hours, one small, puffy white cloud amazingly appeared. Sometimes resting in a tree. Other times sitting atop a hill or a house. When we finally pulled into my friend's driveway, tears came as we celebrated our little clouds along the way, giving us sweet glimpses of God's presence and glory.

Oh, friend, never forget that the same God who met Moses on the mountain, who met my family in the car, is the same God waiting to meet with you!

JOURNAL PROMPT

Accept God's invitation. Find a quiet place to "come" and "be" with God. Stay with Him. Invite Him to show you His light through glimpses of His presence and glory. If you're not sure how to begin, I'm sharing my prayer with you:

> Father, I want to come and be with You . . . to experience more of You. Nurture in me a praying heart that seeks You first in all things. Give me a desire for more of Your presence. Open my eyes to see more of Your glory. Give me ears to hear Your Word when You speak to me. Lord, throughout my day, show me precious glimpses of Your presence and glory. I ask this in Jesus' name. Amen.

9

The Reflected Radiance of God

STACY J. LOWE

As Moses descended from Mount Sinai—with the two tablets of the testimony in his hands as he descended the mountain—he did not realize that the skin of his face shone as a result of his speaking with the Lord.

EXODUS 34:29

Something's different about her! I thought as I watched my friend onstage. Over the year I'd known her, I'd witnessed her growth as a fledgling sign language interpreter. But on this day, she interpreted the opening at church with a confidence and ease I had never seen.

What happened? I wondered.

Turned out, she had spent several weeks soaking up every possible opportunity to attend workshops, discuss interpreting, and observe and learn from others. And it showed.

How and with whom we spend our time will *always* have an outward effect for others to see.

This reminds me of the Old Testament account of Moses returning to the Israelites after fasting for forty days and nights on a mountaintop. During this time away, he received instructions from the Lord (what we know as the Ten Commandments) to share with God's people. Scripture then tells us:

> As Moses descended from Mount Sinai—with the two tablets of the testimony in his hands as he descended the mountain—he did not realize that the skin of his face shone as a result of his speaking with the Lord. (Exodus 34:29)

Can you imagine the awe the Israelites must have felt? Not because of Moses himself but because of what they saw *on* him: God's glory radiating to such a degree they were scared to go near him.

While there's so much we can take from this story, what I love the most is that Moses was completely unaware of his glowing face. That glow was the passive result of an active choice he made to spend time with God, and everyone saw it. How amazingly real the Lord must have been to them in that moment!

That's how incredible our God is. He is so full of light and wonder and majesty that simply being in His presence is enough to change us so that others can see Him.

The more we read His Word, pray, seek His face, and open ourselves to His leading, the more our old patterns and ways of thinking will give way to *His* thoughts and *His* ways, putting Him ever more on display to the world around us.

While it may not be a physical radiance as with Moses, something should be different in our lives for others to notice, so when they're with us, they sense the glory of God. You see, the glow on Moses' face as he descended Mount Sinai was never about him at all. It was always and only about the One in whose presence he'd been. And so it is with us.

When others look at you, what do they see? If you're actively spending time in the presence of God, it just may be His reflected radiance shining back.

JOURNAL PROMPT

When you think of seeing the glory of God in others, who comes to mind? What attributes of God do you see on display in that person, and how can you cultivate those attributes for others to see in you?

_____

_____

_____

_____

_____

_____

_____

_____

_____

10
When We're Standing on Holy Ground

CAROLE HOLIDAY

All the Israelites were watching when the fire descended and the glory of the Lord came on the temple. They bowed down on the pavement with their faces to the ground. They worshiped and praised the Lord: For he is good, for his faithful love endures forever.

2 CHRONICLES 7:3

There's something appropriate about lying prostrate on the ground before the Lord of the universe at the revelation of His presence. I understood that as I fell to my face in utter abandonment. Not in a sanctified space like Solomon's temple but in the carpeted confines of my closet.

It had been a week since my husband had walked out on our marriage, and

I sought refuge in this personal hideaway. My body's posture testified to my desire for God's sovereign will to reign in my life.

A metaphorical fire had decimated my world, yet I sensed that I was occupying holy ground. A place where God would show His supernatural willingness to dwell with me and ultimately to display His glory. His light.

The Bible records examples of God revealing Himself to His people, and one remarkable story is found in 2 Chronicles 7, when King Solomon dedicated the temple. The chapter describes fire descending and filling the temple, reminding Israel of a basic characteristic of God: Where God dwells, light dwells.

God's presence filled the space to the exclusion of anything else . . . an overwhelming brilliance preventing even the Israelites' priests from entering the glowing grounds.

That same fire devoured a sacrifice of livestock that day. King Solomon offered up thousands from his herds to the Lord to sanctify the space. A fiery exclamation point to the dedication of the temple.

It's hard for me to imagine that scene. It is not, however, hard to imagine the response to that scene: Hit the deck. Face to the dirt. Eyes covered to block the brilliance. Wherever God's light is shining, it triggers a deferential posture within His people. I believe the witnesses that day took a posture expressing utter abandonment to their desire for God's sovereign presence to reign in their lives. Just like I did in that carpeted closet.

And where did that lead them?

After the terror of that fire, the Bible reveals that once the people fell to their faces, they celebrated and left "rejoicing and with happy hearts" (2 Chronicles 7:10). Their music celebrated God's goodness and His faithful love with the instruments of David accompanying their songs.

Reverence. Abandonment. Awe. Wonder. Worship. Rejoicing. God's glory in the glow of His light.

The natural order of things in the most supernatural circumstances. The same order I experienced that day of fire in my closet. And the same order you can experience when the fires of life sweep through your world. They can lead you to sing of God's goodness and His faithful love, which endures for generations.

JOURNAL PROMPT

Read other scriptures where the people of God fell on their faces in response to God's luminous presence. Note the ways God's presence was demonstrated by different kinds of light.

Ezekiel 1:25–28
Daniel 10:1–9

11

God Shines a Flashlight to Guide Our Souls

DORINA LAZO GILMORE-YOUNG

Send your light and your truth; let them lead me. Let them bring me to your holy mountain, to your dwelling place. Then I will come to the altar of God, to God, my greatest joy. I will praise you with the lyre, God, my God.

PSALM 43:3–4

When I was little, my parents took us camping for most of our family vacations. There's something glorious and gritty about setting up a tent and sleeping beneath a star-studded sky. To help us feel safe, my dad made sure we each had our own flashlight by our pillows in case we needed some light in the middle of the night.

Our flashlights were small, but my dad kept a huge one that could light up the whole tent or the pathway to the bathroom if we needed it. I always felt safe with my dad and his flashlight nearby.

As grateful as I am for flashlights to help illuminate, guide, and provide security, they are incomparable to the power of God's light. The writer of Psalm 43:3 recognized this power and wrote, "Send your light and your truth; let them lead me. Let them bring me to your holy mountain, to your dwelling place."

The psalmist expressed a personal heart prayer that is full of longing for restoration into God's presence. He wrote honestly, asking God for guidance because he felt distant from God and longed for the light to illuminate the path of his life. I resonate deeply with the honest questions and lament in the words of Psalm 43. When my husband died from cancer ten years ago, leaving me a widowed mama to three young girls, I cried out to God with a similar kind of longing. The days felt long and dark. My grief felt heavy and confusing, shadowing my heart like clouds covering the stars at night.

I had to trust God with our present and our future when it seemed I was surrounded by darkness.

But I discovered in those days that God is our light through dark seasons of the soul. I learned that I could build my trust in God by reminding myself of His character like the psalmist did. Psalm 43:1–4 reminds us that God defends, rescues, and provides refuge. He is the true source of light, truth, and joy. He can shine His light to navigate tough decisions and traverse trying times. When I was unsure of myself, I asked God to shine light on our situation or give me a creative solution as a parent. When our finances weren't adding up, I prayed for God to provide glimmers of hope. He always did this in surprising ways.

Psalm 43:4 is also an invitation to return to praise: "Then I will come to the altar of God, to God, my greatest joy. I will praise you with the lyre, God, my God." The psalmist hoped to return to the presence of God, where he could experience joy and worship.

No matter our dark circumstances, God reveals Himself in light. We can put our hope in Him and praise Him, knowing He will light our way.

JOURNAL PROMPT

Have you ever experienced a dark season in your life? How did God provide light in that season? Can you tell someone about what you experienced and how God revealed Himself to you?

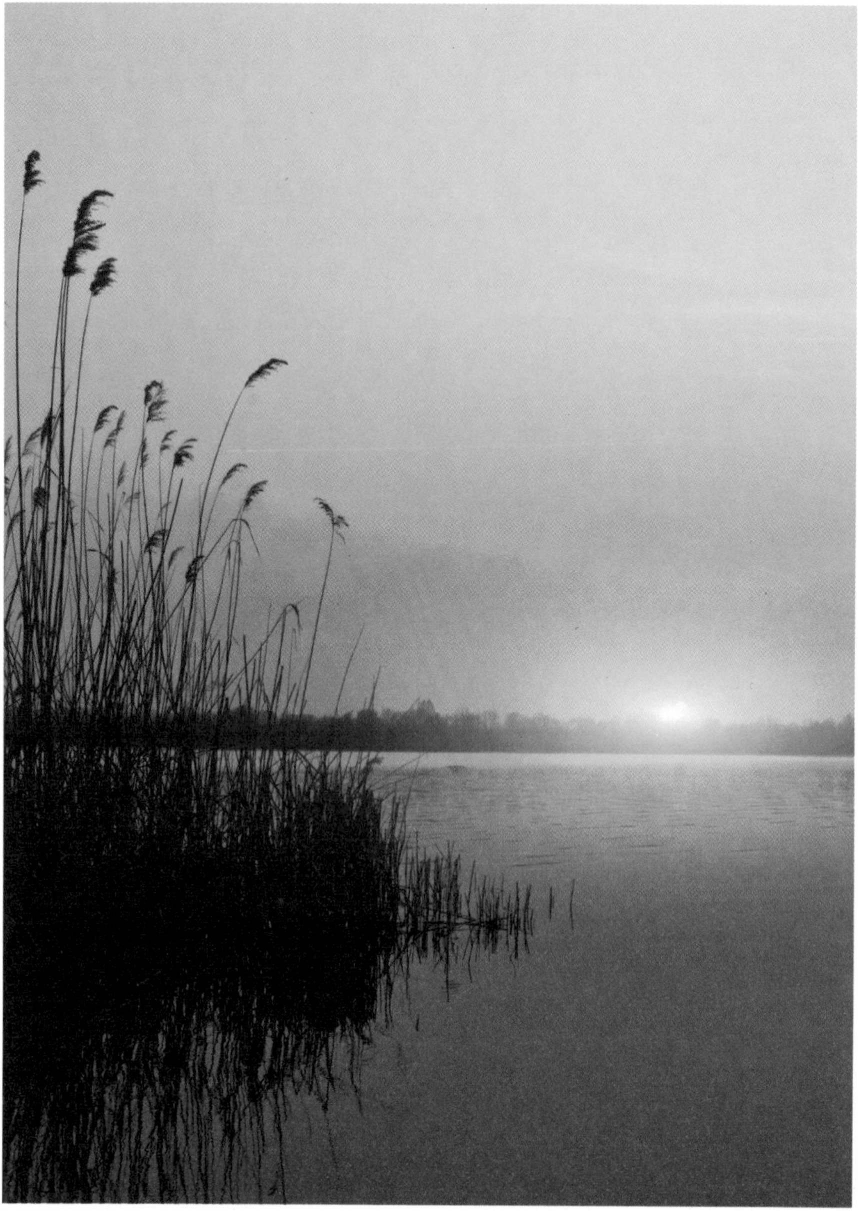

PART 3

We Have Walked in Darkness

We were never meant to walk in darkness. But sin separated us from God's presence, and we have turned from the light of His face to pursue our own will. The good news is that even in the darkest places, God still pursues us. There is no place too dark, because wherever God is, light is there too.

12

Walk in the Light as He Is in the Light

DR. AVRIL OCCILIEN-SIMILIEN

This is the message we have heard from him and declare to you: God is light, and there is absolutely no darkness in him. If we say, "We have fellowship with him," and yet we walk in darkness, we are lying and are not practicing the truth. If we walk in the light as he himself is in the light, we have fellowship with one another, and the blood of Jesus his Son cleanses us from all sin.

1 JOHN 1:5–7

I sat in the dark, a flashlight's beam my only source of light. I heard the air-conditioning click on and felt the air begin to wisp against my skin. The power lost during the recent storm had finally returned. As I used the flashlight to navigate across the room to the light switch, I was struck by the difference between these two sources of light.

The flashlight offered control over which small areas of the room were illuminated, but I was still walking in a room that was mostly dark. When I flipped the light switch, the entire room lit up, eliminating the darkness and allowing me to walk fully in the light.

At that moment, I was reminded of 1 John 1:5–7, which prompts us: "This is the message we have heard from him and declare to you: God is light, and there is absolutely no darkness in him. If we say, 'We have fellowship with him,' and yet we walk in darkness, we are lying and are not practicing the truth. If we walk in the light as he himself is in the light, we have fellowship with one another, and the blood of Jesus his Son cleanses us from all sin."

Then the analogy became clear. The contrast between the flashlight and the ceiling light reminded me of my need to surrender to God's guidance, to allow His light to illuminate *every* area of my life.

Sometimes it's easy to live like we're using a spiritual flashlight—shining God's light only on certain aspects of our lives while keeping others hidden in darkness. But God calls us to flip the switch, to allow His light to fill every corner of our beings.

How do we walk in the light? How do we transform the dark areas of our lives into places filled with light and life? We do so by cultivating a heart of surrender through prayer and soaking in the Word of God daily. The more we allow God's Word to penetrate our hearts, the more our lives reflect His light. Jesus declared, "I am the light of the world. Anyone who follows me will never walk in the darkness but will have the light of life" (John 8:12).

Friend, are there areas of your life that seem to be in the dark? Areas where doubt, fear, anxiety, lack, or disappointment cast a shadow? Perhaps you have hesitated to bring these struggles into the light, unsure of the result of fully surrendering them to God. But remember, God wants it all. He desires our complete surrender.

As you continue this journey of faith, I encourage you to surrender fully to God's work in your life. Allow Him to shine His light into those dark areas, to bring healing, clarity, and peace. Walk in the light as He is in the light, and experience the fullness of life that only He can give.

JOURNAL PROMPT

What areas of your life seem overshadowed by doubt, fear, anxiety, lack, or disappointment? What scriptures speak to those parts of life? Pray that as God illuminates these parts of your life, you will fully surrender to His work.

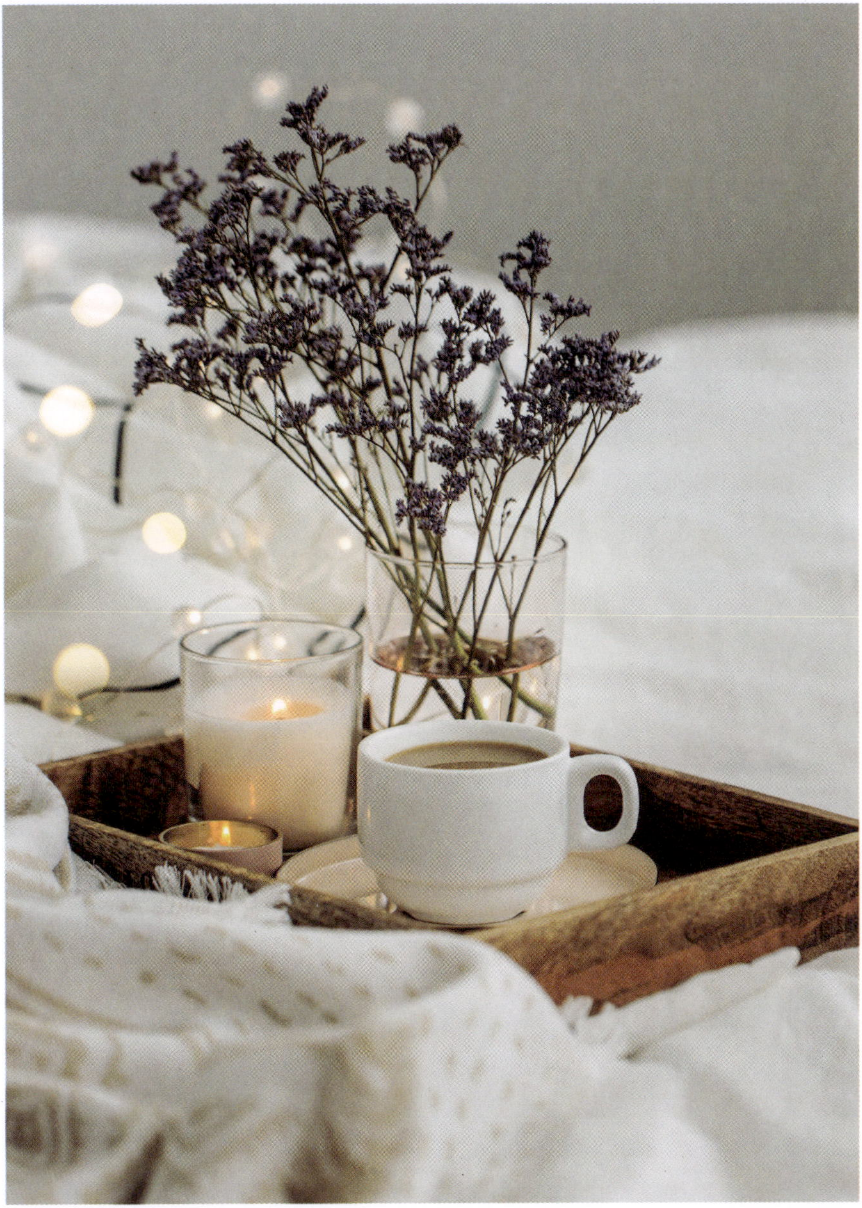

13

A Wing and a Prayer

CLAIRE FOXX

This is the judgment: The light has come into the world, and people loved darkness rather than the light because their deeds were evil.

JOHN 3:19

I have a friend who hates bugs. In a big way.

In fact, a few summers ago, she bought her own personal bug zapper. Once a week, we sat outside together for evening Bible study, and around sunset she'd unzip her bag and take out the battery-powered device. It was a little bigger than a Ping-Pong paddle and buzzed with an electric charge when "armed." Any moths or mosquitoes that flew too close . . . well, their flying days were over.

"It's self-defense!" she said. But the zapper had an offensive mode, too, featuring a bluish light that attracted insects to their demise.

Nocturnal insects are instinctively drawn to light. They can't help it.

They'll fly into a fire (or an electrified Ping-Pong paddle, let's say) because they can't resist that seemingly inviting glow.

I couldn't resist poking fun at my friend's extraordinary measures, but I'll admit I felt a little bad for the bugs. After all, I can relate to messed-up instincts and misguided impulses. I've been zapped a time or two.

How about you?

For us humans, the problem isn't that we are instinctively drawn to light—it's that we are drawn to darkness. As John 3:19 says, "The light has come into the world, and people loved darkness rather than the light because their deeds were evil."

It's a fatal attraction: Against all better judgment, like moths to a flame, we fly toward what is harmful instead of helpful, greedy instead of good, selfish instead of righteous. We disobey the God who knows what's best for us. Sometimes we're oblivious to the danger, but other times we're well aware—and we still do the wrong thing. We *love* disobedience.

And we have an enemy who gladly uses every kind of sinful lure, trap, snare, and zapper he can think of to exterminate us. Satan's dark devices of temptation are designed to make evil seem irresistible—to convince us we're no better than the bugs. Foolish and flammable. Broken and burned.

Zap.

Thankfully, though, that's not where the story ends.

Yes, our hearts are drawn to darkness. Yes, our deeds can be evil. Yes, our Enemy is a cunning exterminator. But we have a God who has defeated darkness, evil, and the Enemy—in a big way.

He declares:

"Anyone who follows me will never walk in the darkness" (John 8:12).

"The darkness did not overcome [the light]" (John 1:5).

"Anyone who believes in [Me] is not condemned" (John 3:18).

And unlike the Enemy, God speaks only the truth.

So we can trust God when He tells us the good news: Jesus is not only "the light [who came] into the world" but the Savior who went to the cross to lay down His life for sinners like you and me (John 3:19). Surely there is no darkness darker than the grave where Jesus lay shrouded for three days. Yet when He rolled away that stone, Sunday-morning sunlight chased away every shadow of death, and what was once a burial chamber became a beacon of hope for all who will believe.

The tomb is empty! And the same Holy Spirit who raised Jesus from the dead is the one who opens our eyes to see that He came not to condemn us for our dark desires but to save us from them forever.

His hope shines today, tomorrow, and always—no batteries required.

JOURNAL PROMPT

How does the empty tomb change your perspective on the judgment mentioned in John 3:19? How has faith in Jesus transformed your own heart's desires from darkness to light?

_____

_____

_____

_____

_____

_____

_____

14

The Lasting Light in Our Lamps

JUNE CHAPMAN

The eye is the lamp of the body. If your eye is healthy, your whole body will be full of light. But if your eye is bad, your whole body will be full of darkness. So if the light within you is darkness, how deep is that darkness!

MATTHEW 6:22–23

My first significant dream was shattered when I was a teenager. I'd worked hard through grade school to achieve an award I thought would make me happy. Friends would see my success, my family would be proud, and my efforts would be recognized. I prepared myself for the honor of hearing my name over the speakers. But something unexpected happened. A different name was announced. Someone else had won.

I froze, crushed with confusion and shame. How had it all gone so wrong? It might not seem like much now, but that award was my whole world then.

I had set my sights on the thing I thought would satisfy me, but it could not bear the weight of my expectations.

In the Sermon on the Mount, Jesus warned of the danger of the misguided gaze:

> The eye is the lamp of the body. If your eye is healthy, your whole body will be full of light. But if your eye is bad, your whole body will be full of darkness. So if the light within you is darkness, how deep is that darkness! (Matthew 6:22–23)

The light in our "lamps" determines the health of our spiritual lives. Our eyes will let in either artificial light or lasting light. When we seek Jesus first, we are filled with the sustaining light of life, and we cultivate our treasure in Him. But when we find our treasure elsewhere, we're drawn to artificial light that can't provide what it promises. It can't satisfy or sustain. And it has a dark secret. Even when it fills us, we're left wanting more. It erodes our attention one glance at a time.

The Enemy longs for us to underestimate the ability of the objects of our affection to distract us. His goal is to steal one precious thing: our devotion. Our eyes almost imperceptibly build our idols. Those objects, in turn, gain the power to guide us. When we allow the wrong things to light up our lives, we put our hope in fraudulent places, pointing our hearts in fruitless directions. The light within us is then darkness, and it is doubly thick, as our hearts descend into deadly distraction.

We will be drawn to what we behold; gazing on waste lays waste to the soul.

Our affections grow toward the light we let inside. To draw close to the lasting light of Christ, we must keep our eyes on Him, intentionally placing Him above our worldly desires. He will give us strength as we resolve to worship Him first. The eye is never satisfied with worldly things, but Jesus is enough to fill the darkened void.

All the awards in the world could not sustain my soul. My true confidence is not carved on the nameplates of trophies. In fact, it isn't earned at all. It's found in the lasting light that sustains my soul, in the One who gave freely the salvation I could never win onstage. In Him I find a title worth far more than what I lost in grade school: daughter of the King.

In a world that threatens to steal our hearts, Jesus delights in meeting us with the light of His mercy. Our expectations of His goodness are never misguided. His is the lasting light that freely invites and fully satisfies.

JOURNAL PROMPT

What treasures occupy your thoughts, attention, and affection? Is there anything (or anyone) that, if taken away, would cause you to doubt God's goodness or His love for you? Think through these questions and ask the Lord to help direct your devotion to Him alone, storing up your richest treasure in heaven.

_____

_____

_____

_____

_____

_____

_____

15

Our God of (Im)Possible

MEGHAN MELLINGER

*He reveals the deep and hidden things; he knows
what is in the darkness, and light dwells with him.*

DANIEL 2:22

Pretend for a minute that you're Daniel from the Bible. You're not stuck in a den with lions (yet!), but your life is in danger.

You've been plucked from your fallen homeland of Jerusalem for a three-year boot camp to learn the ways of your new oppressors in Babylon: the largest city in the world at its peak of splendor—and darkness. A city known for its power and its sin.

Babylon's king, Nebuchadnezzar, is deeply troubled. He had a dream he couldn't make sense of and called upon his local magicians and sorcerers not only to interpret his dream but first to reveal what the dream was. It was an impossible task they could not perform—so the unhappy king issued a decree to kill all the wise men in Babylon.

That means you, too, because the Lord has gifted you with wisdom and knowledge not only of language and literature but of dreams and visions.

So you step out in faith and ask for an audience with the king before you even know what the dream was. But why such a bold move when your life, and many others', are at stake?

Because the king and his wise men walk in darkness, but you know the God of light:

> [God] reveals the deep and hidden things; he knows what is in the darkness, and light dwells with him. (Daniel 2:22)

God revealed the king's dream to Daniel so he could stand confidently and declare, "No wise man, medium, magician, or diviner is able to make known to the king the mystery he asked about. But there is a God in heaven who reveals mysteries, and he has let King Nebuchadnezzar know what will happen in the last days" (vv. 2:27–28).

What was impossible to men was possible with our God.

Our lives might not depend on us interpreting a king's dream anytime soon, but we can learn a couple of things from Daniel.

Daniel kept his eyes on the King of kings in the middle of Babylon's darkness. He didn't eat Nebuchadnezzar's food or bow to his idols (1:8). He remained steadfast to our good God, and God rewarded Daniel's faithfulness with wisdom.

We still live in Babylon, a world at the peak of splendor—and darkness. We think ourselves progressive and advanced with so much available at our fingertips, yet we're living in a kingdom just as dark and troubled. But we can choose to keep our eyes, minds, and lives fixed on our God of light and His ways.

God is still in the business of revealing mysteries to His people. What was impossible for those walking without God is possible for those walking closely with Him. Our God knows the depths of our world and the depths of our hearts. This shouldn't be scary; it should be comforting. Nothing is too much or too strange or too heavy for our relational and loving God. He cares about us too much to leave us in darkness.

So pretend for a minute that you're Daniel from the Bible, and walk with your eyes fixed on the God of light who won't let you walk in darkness.

JOURNAL PROMPT

In what ways do you feel God might be calling you to honor Him through your daily living in this dark world?

_____

_____

_____

_____

_____

_____

_____

_____

_____

_____

16

The Silent Rhythm of Life

DR. ALICIA BRITT CHOLE

You set all the boundaries of the earth; you made summer and winter.

PSALM 74:17

A century ago, a few fragile seeds fell upon rocky soil. Through drought and flood, they clung tightly to earth, stubbornly stretching toward the heavens. Today silver maple, post oak, and black walnut trees surround our home like tall, loyal sentinels, reaching to the light.

Though my skin prefers their role in summer, when they grant me relief from the hot sun, somehow my soul prefers their lessons in winter. It is then, when growth pauses, that the trees have often become my teachers.

What the plenty of summer hides, the nakedness of winter reveals: infrastructure. (Fullness often distracts from foundations.)

In the stillness of winter, the trees' true strength is unveiled. Stripped of decoration, the tree trunks become prominent.

As a child, I always colored tree trunks brown, but to my adult eyes, they appear to be more of a warm gray. Starting with their thick bases, I begin studying each tree. Buckling strips of bark clothe foot after foot of weathered branches. Leafless, the trees feature their intricate support systems. Detail is visible, as is dead wood. Lifeless limbs concealed by summer's boasting are now exposed.

In winter, are the trees bare? Yes.

In winter, are the trees barren? No.

Life still is.

Life does not sleep—though in winter, she retracts all advertisement. And when she does so, she is conserving and preparing for the future.

And so it is with us. Seasonally, we, too, are stripped of visible fruit. Our giftings are hidden; our abilities are underestimated. When previous successes fade and current efforts falter, we can easily mistake our fruitlessness for failure.

But such is the rhythm of spiritual life: new growth, fruitfulness, transition, rest . . . new growth, fruitfulness, transition, rest. Abundance may make us feel more productive, but perhaps emptiness has greater power to strengthen our souls.

In spiritual winters, our fullness is thinned so that, undistracted by our giftings, we can focus on our character. In the absence of anything to measure, we are left with nothing to stare at except our foundation.

Risking inspection, we begin to examine the motivations that support our deeds, the attitudes that influence our words, the deadwood otherwise hidden beneath our busyness. Then a life-changing transition occurs as we move from resistance through repentance to the place of rest. With gratitude, we simply abide.

Like a tree planted by living water, thriving in the sunshine, we focus on our primary responsibility: remaining in Christ.

In winter, are we bare? Yes.

In winter, are we barren? No.

True life still is.

The Father's work in us does not sleep—although in spiritual winters He retracts all advertisement. And when He does so, He is purifying our faith, strengthening our character, conserving our energy, and preparing us for the future.

The sleepy days of winter hide us so that the seductive days of summer will not ruin us.

<small>Adapted from *Anonymous: Jesus' Hidden Years...and Yours* by Alicia Britt Chole (Thomas Nelson, 2011), used with permission.</small>

JOURNAL PROMPT

As you look back at the spiritual winters of your life, what aspect of your character did God develop?

_____

_____

_____

_____

_____

_____

_____

_____

_____

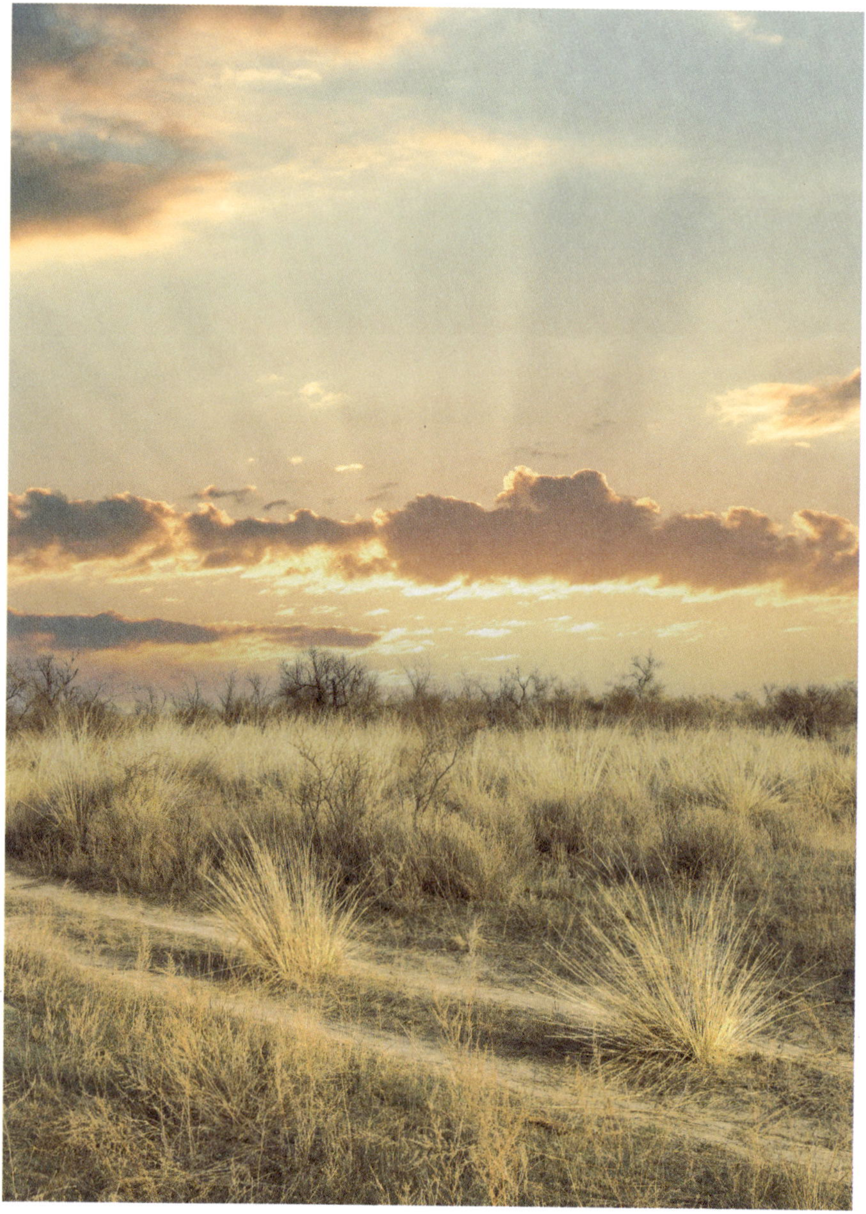

PART 4

God's Blessings Shine

The prophet Isaiah declared that God's justice would be "a light to the nations" (Isaiah 51:4). The psalmist declared that God would light the path for the righteous (Psalm 119:105). Our covenant God is always faithful to provide blessings that shine on our lives. They might not be "spotlight" blessings, but we can be sure there will be enough light for the next step.

17

Whose Light Is It Anyway?

CLAIRE FOXX

Pay attention to me, my people, and listen to me, my nation; for instruction will come from me, and my justice for a light to the nations. I will bring it about quickly.

ISAIAH 51:4

For a stretch of my childhood, I shared a bedroom with my stepsister. During those years, we fought over the lamp.

There was only one in the bedroom: single light bulb, yellow ceramic base, fringed linen shade. We used it as a night-light. When the sun went down, we'd pick up our ongoing argument over who would get to sleep with the lamp on her bedside table.

"You had it yesterday!"

"I had a bad dream, so I need it tonight."

"Mom said I could."

"Remember when you left it on all day while we were at school? That's a waste of energy. I always turn it off."

"Dibs! I called dibs! You can't call dibs after I *already* called dibs."

We'd pull out our résumés as the clock struck nine and list all the qualifications and extenuating circumstances that made us each uniquely worthy of the light.

Maybe the people of ancient Israel felt similarly when they heard the Lord say, "Pay attention to me, my people, and listen to me, my nation; for instruction will come from me, and my justice for a light" (Isaiah 51:4).

Israel was *God's* nation. *His* people were set apart for *His* holy purposes. Surely God's promised instruction would bring them unique blessings and special insights not available to anyone else in the world!

Imagine when the Israelites heard the rest of Isaiah 51:4: "For instruction will come from me, and my justice for a light *to the nations*. I will bring it about quickly" (italics added).

A light to . . . who?

When the prophet Isaiah delivered these words from the Lord, Israel had been invaded and exiled by the nation of Assyria (Isaiah 36). They called out to other nations like Egypt for help, but it did no good (Isaiah 31). In other words, "the nations" were no friends of God's people. Their spiritual résumé was filled with destruction and darkness.

But God didn't say the nations were worthy of His light. For that matter, He didn't say Israel was worthy either.

God simply promised His justice would shine.

A couple of verses earlier, in Isaiah 51:2, God told His people, "Look to Abraham your father." This takes us back to Genesis 12:1–3, where God first declared that He would make Abraham's family into the "great nation" of Israel—and that "all the peoples on earth will be blessed through [Israel]."

God indeed spoke His life-giving laws to the Israelites, but His word would also shine *through* them and *beyond* them, revealing His ways to the whole world. And as He dealt justly with both Israel and the nations that oppressed them in Isaiah's day, God's radiant righteousness would be displayed to all people.

The truth is that none of us is worthy of God's redeeming light in our lives—but we sure do need it. And our God sure is good. Despite our darkness, He promises, "My salvation appears, and my arms will bring justice to the nations. The coasts and islands will put their hope in me" (Isaiah 51:5).

So when our own pride tempts us to defend, debate, or doubt where we think the Lord should plug in His lamp . . . let's remember Isaiah and leave the light of the world up to Him.

When we put down our résumés and our arguments about who is worthy of the light, we might be surprised to discover what I eventually did in my childhood bedroom: That small yellow lamp was enough to brighten every dark night, no matter whose table it was on.

JOURNAL PROMPT

What people or situations in your life tempt you to question God's justice? How does it bring you peace to remember that God is both just and gracious in shining His light on the whole world?

_____

_____

_____

_____

_____

18

Just Enough Light for the Next Step

MEGHAN MELLINGER

Your word is a lamp for my feet and a light on my path.
PSALM 119:105

I don't think I could get anywhere without the Maps application on my phone. This crystal ball of roadways tells me everything I want to know: What's the best way to get where I'm going? Will I run into any obstacles? How long will the trip take?

The only problem left is whether to choose a British or an Australian voice as my tour guide.

If only I had an app for my life to tell me everything I want to know: What route should I take to meet the right guy? How many options do I have in a career? How many trials can I expect if I go this direction?

But instead, navigating my life feels like standing in the forest. In the dark. On an unmarked path. Alone with no phone. I don't know what or how many obstacles are ahead. *How far till the end? Do I have enough snacks? What just touched my leg?*

But then I look down at my hands, and there's a small light.

It's not a huge torch or a high-powered flashlight. No—it's a small candle with a single wick.

It's not enough to illuminate a half mile down the path, but it's just enough to take the next step.

And the next.

And the next.

That's what our heavenly Navigator does for us. He doesn't promise to reveal the entire journey to us all at once, but He does promise to light up our next step.

> [God's] word is a lamp for my feet and a light on my path. (Psalm 119:105)

The Bible is our resource, our map, our guiding light. I might not know if I'll get married, but the Bible tells me the qualities to look for in a godly spouse and how to spend the time I have wisely. I might not know what my next job will be, but His Word tells me how important it is to use my gifts and talents to glorify Him. I might not know how many trials are up ahead, but Scripture tells me God's promises for me in the midst of them.

I won't know everything that's ahead, but I know the One who does.

In our world of instant gratification and answers without delay, we are called to trust. To release the reins and relish in the right now. Because when we let God's wisdom for life guide us, we don't have to stress or fret or fear what's ahead. Each step is a chance to experience His presence, power, and promise.

With God's Word as our light, we are armed with knowledge. Not enough to know it all but enough to know the next step. God will illuminate all areas of our lives and guide us forward, one faithful step at a time.

And before we know it, we'll be well on our way down the road.

JOURNAL PROMPT

Today, what area of your life can you entrust to God for the next small step?

19

God Is Still Good

HADASSAH TREU

L̲o̲r̲d̲, you light my lamp; my God illuminates my darkness.
PSALM 18:28

The first minute after I wake up is the hardest. I only want to close my eyes again and go back to the land of dreams, refusing to face the painful reality of how life turned out after the unexpected loss that plunged me into darkness.

I don't know what darkness you are facing today, but I imagine you feel alone. Perhaps it's the loss of a job, the illness of a loved one, the disillusionment from shattered dreams, or the struggle that comes with depression or habitual sin. Maybe it's the sting of betrayal or the uncertainty of the future weighing heavily over you.

Every morning since my life turned upside down, when my feet touch the floor, I remind myself that I am not left alone in the darkness.

King David experienced darkness and loneliness in the form of prolonged persecution, isolation, false accusation, and suffering. Yet the Lord sustained him, delivered him from all his enemies, and gave him a place of honor.

After God rescued and delivered David from the hands of his enemies, David penned these words of praise and victory: "Lord, you light my lamp; my God illuminates my darkness" (Psalm 18:28).

And today the Lord still lights my lamp and illuminates my darkness. He is willing and able to carry me through when I can't see the way.

When we are in the darkness of suffering and pain, we can doubt God's goodness and favor toward us. We struggle to process and accept our circumstances and wonder why God allowed this or that to happen. But our painful feelings don't tell the truth about God's character. God is good, and He has our utmost good in mind while dealing with us. It is difficult to reconcile suffering with the heart of our loving God, but as long as we live in the flesh, suffering and struggle will be part of our earthly lives.

This is why it's important to remember that Jesus has overcome the world; He has overcome the darkness, and He can overcome *our* darkness because He is the Light of the World.

The Lord illuminates our darkness by reminding us of His truths and wonderful promises and by nourishing and sustaining us daily through His indwelling Spirit. He helps change our perspectives and gives wisdom and understanding. He takes care of us, meets our needs, and provides grace and help every day by bringing people and resources to our aid.

The Lord breathes life into our weary souls and woos us to draw near and trust Him, making us capable of enduring until this season is over. He comes even closer in the darkness, revealing hidden treasures of heavenly wisdom. The God of all comfort and the Redeemer of our losses collects every tear and numbers all our steps. He is near and He cares.

When we are in darkness, we are blessed to receive the special comfort of God's most tender presence and care.

JOURNAL PROMPT

What darkness are you facing now or have faced recently? In what ways has the Lord illuminated your darkness? What has He shown you and taught you? Reflect on all the blessings you've experienced in this period of your life, and thank the Lord for them.

_____

_____

_____

_____

_____

_____

_____

_____

_____

_____

_____

_____

_____

20

The Brightly Lit Path

CAROLE HOLIDAY

*The path of the righteous is like the light of dawn,
shining brighter and brighter until midday.
But the way of the wicked is like the darkest gloom;
they don't know what makes them stumble.*

PROVERBS 4:18–19

I am not a morning person.

However, the times I *have* seen the sun rise have been magical. And I wonder why I don't get up earlier. The appeal of dawn is its promise . . . the golden rays of first light signal a new beginning and an accompanying outlook that leaves me hopeful with anticipation. I know there is more to come. It's God's daily dose of fresh starts.

In Proverbs 4, Solomon made promises about paths washed by the light of dawn. Not to everyone, however. As is his literary style, the legendary king often contrasted wise and foolish, and in this passage, the righteous and the not-so-righteous. He's known for drawing a line in the sand with a sharp stick.

These two groups, the righteous and the wicked, travel on divergent paths, indicating that there will be a choice to make. A fork-in-the-road moment or two. One way will be well lit, and the other will grow dimmer, obscuring obstacles in the path.

Solomon, reflecting on lessons learned from his own father, King David, taught a master class on wisdom in Proverbs 4. He urged his students to follow the illuminated path, instructing them to avoid the pitfalls of the darkened way (vv. 11–19).

The warning of dimly lit pathways brings to my mind a July afternoon when a much-anticipated white water rafting trip turned into a near disaster. En route to the river's launching point, our small plane roughly navigated an emergency landing, and four friends and I found ourselves stumbling through the darkening Idaho wilderness. Our goal was to reach an abandoned hunting camp. Only our pilot knew the way.

Never have I listened so closely to another's words. Familiar with the terrain and aware of the forest's dangers, this experienced guide offered instructions to get us safely to our destination. I was terrified but felt braver when I stuck closely behind him, able to navigate the roots and rocks by modeling his steps.

Never had I wished more for the midday sun.

This is what Solomon had in mind, clearly explaining that following God's ordinances is like following God's voice as a trusted guide. The righteous, who listen and live according to His Word, will be rewarded with a well-lit path allowing for safety, vision, and progress. The same hopeful outlook that accompanies dawn will accompany their steps with the added blessing of light "shining brighter and brighter until midday" (v.18).

The wise king used a common illustration that everyone could understand:

The midday sun offers warmth, comfort, and a clear path ahead. When the sun reaches its highest point in the sky, its light is the brightest, and shadows are the shortest. What could hide from us then?

Today, if you don't know the way to go, Solomon's instruction is clear. Listen to the teachings of God, and follow their prompting. Let the word *righteous* describe your life. That path promises to be brightly lit.

JOURNAL PROMPT

Read all of Proverbs 4. Note all the ways Solomon exhorted his audience to seek wisdom. This proverb doesn't reveal *exactly* which way to go—to the right or to the left—but it tells us who to *be* if we want to see a clear path. Focus on that, and trust that the wisest way will be illuminated for you. It is promised to the righteous one.

21

We Bless Him When We Feel Blessed and Even When We Don't

RACHEL MARIE KANG

For they did not take the land by their sword—their arm did not bring them victory—but by your right hand, your arm, and the light of your face, because you were favorable toward them.

PSALM 44:3

I'm the kind of girl who grew up outside, playing house under the branches of our Althea bush and spending hours catching crayfish with my cousins in the creek at my grandma's house.

Lately, though, home and land feel like a song of loss on my lips. I grieve the loss of my grandma's house, which has now been sold. It's still erect, still tucked away behind that long gravel driveway, still kissed by the creek and hugged by those mountains in the backyard. But year after year, I drive by and watch the decline of both that house and the village it was nestled in.

Once hidden away in a small village inhabited by a tight-knit community of kin, my grandmother's house—and that small village—are now crawling with people who care for nothing of the sort. Devastated, our community has watched a people-oriented place become plundered because of its proximity to New York City: houses sold left and right, generations of residents displaced, homes turned into developments, and land—mountains, creeks, historical landmarks—all neglected.

When I first read Psalm 44:3, it stung: "For they did not take the land by their sword—their arm did not bring them victory—but by your right hand, your arm, and the light of your face, because you were favorable toward them." Truth is, I'm the one who wants to take back land by sword. I want to use my every power and effort to go back to the day when all was right in my life and on this land I love.

But then I read the rest of Psalm 44—a psalm of sorrow, lament, and longing. In verse 1, the psalmist began by looking back on God's faithfulness to His people. "Our ancestors have told us," the psalmist wrote. Shortly after, he praised God for His past provision and protection—the blessing found in "the light" of His face (v. 3).

The psalm, however, quickly turns a corner as the psalmist then began to paint a picture of the present-day suffering and devastation of God's people. And that blessing once found in the light of God's face? Surely it was a distant memory, a hand-me-down history. The psalmist cried, "Why do you hide?" (v. 24). *Why has God turned away His face? Why does the light of the Lord no longer shine upon us?*

It got me—the sorrow-filled girl who wants to take back land by sword—thinking.

Is not the Lord still worthy to be praised? Whether He blesses or not? Whether we feel the light of His face shining upon us or not?

Since the fall, all our stories have been stitched in and through with both brokenness and the blessing of God—grief and goodness, hurt and hope, loss and love. Yet in all of this, God is always worthy of our worship. Whether we see or sense His blessings toward us . . . or not. Still, He is due all blessing and praise.

May we bless Him when we feel blessed and even when we don't. May we bless Him for every blessing that *has* come and every blessing *yet* to come.

May we bless Him when He is good. And also? May we bless Him simply because He is God.

JOURNAL PROMPT

Whether your life feels favorable or not, what is one thing you can bless the Lord for?

_____

_____

_____

_____

_____

_____

_____

_____

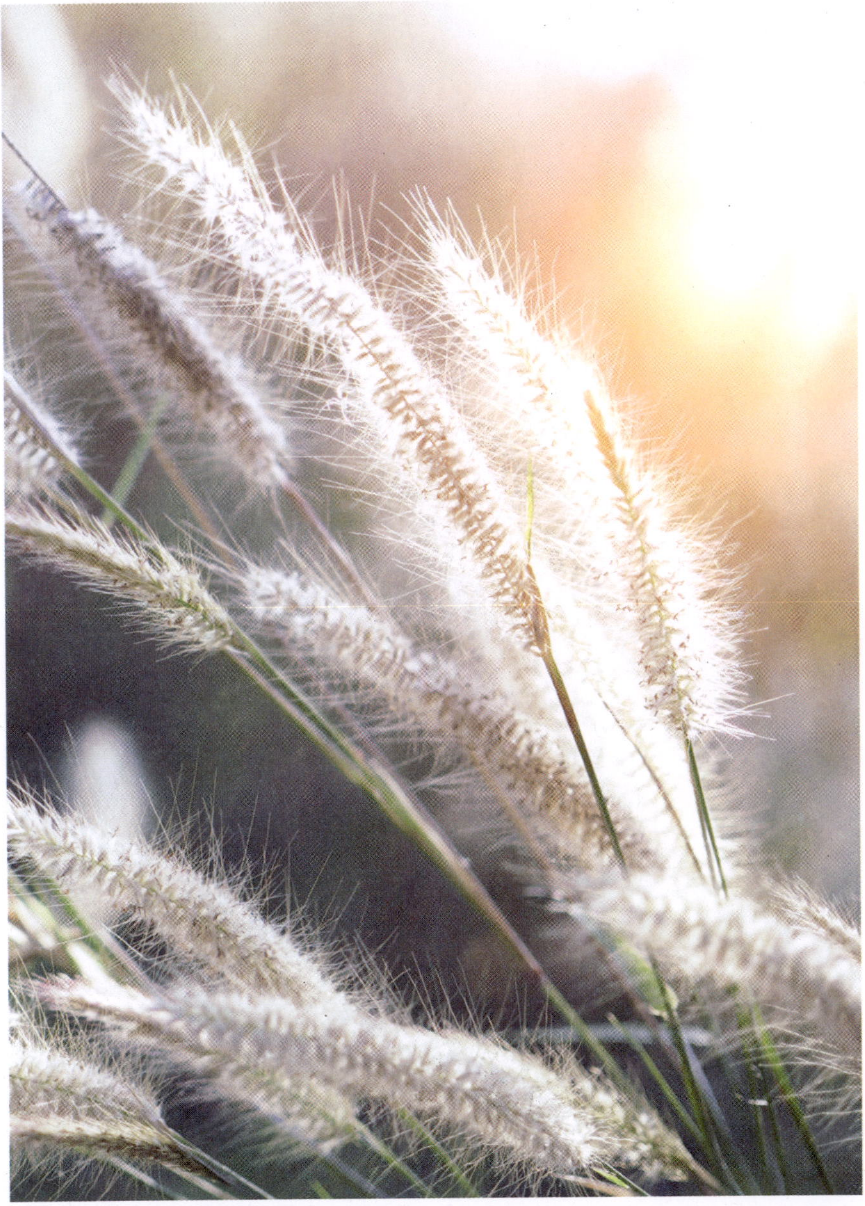

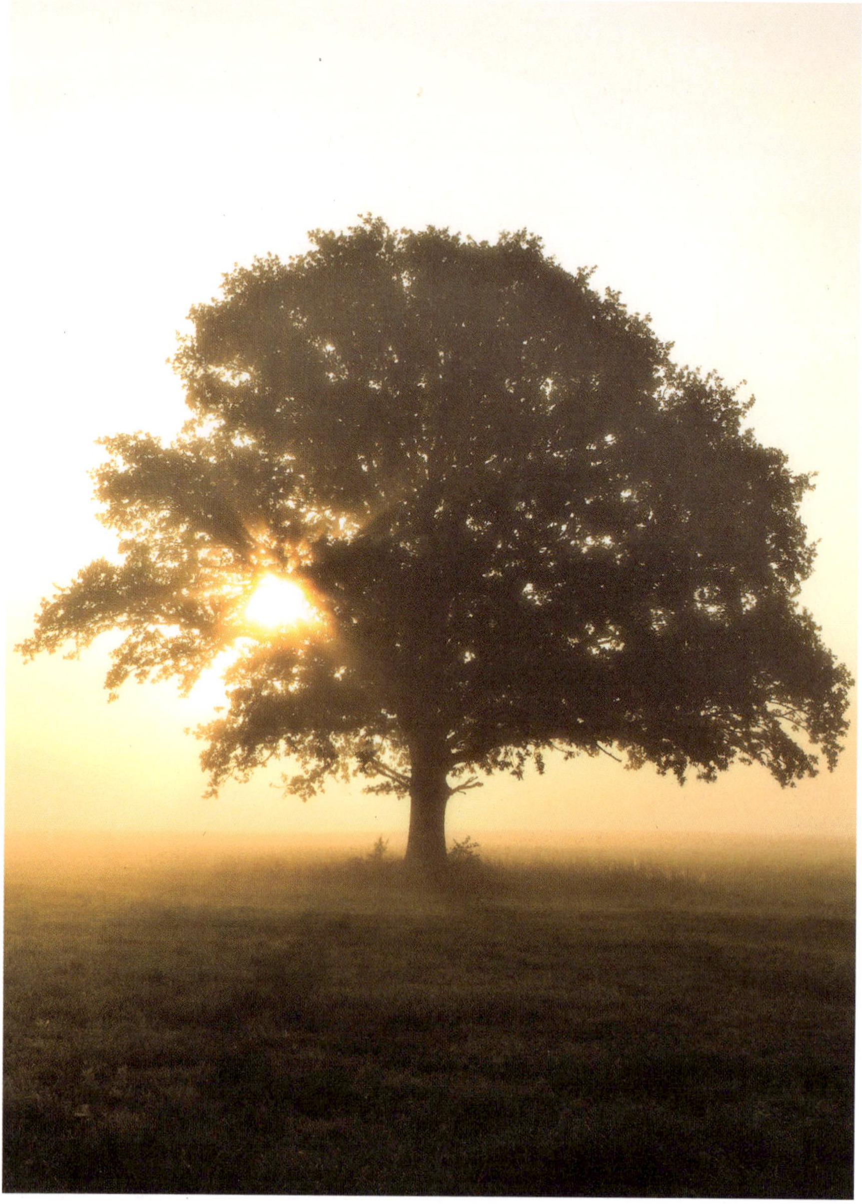

PART 5

Darkness Will Not Last Forever

For those who have walked in dark places for a long time, it can seem that the light will never shine again. But God has promised not to abandon His people. Though we may not see clearly now, God will lead us in new ways, on paths we haven't traveled before, making rough places level and dark places light.

22

Stepping Out of the Shadows

SARAH FREYMUTH

If I say, "Surely the darkness shall cover me, and the light about me be night," even the darkness is not dark to you; the night is bright as the day, for darkness is as light with you.

PSALM 139:11–12 ESV

How did I get here *again*?

Like the line in an old hymn, my heart is prone to wander to places I know I shouldn't go. And yet I dabble in the darkness of envy, pride, and anger until I'm deeply entwined with no way out. The struggle between flesh and spirit leaves me shadowed in shame. Can I let God see me like this?

Whether we've stumbled or sprinted toward things in life that prove harmful, we can be tempted to draw back into the shadows and hide our faces from God. We don't want Him to see us like this: broken, bruised, and bewildered.

Wouldn't it be better if He didn't have to look at the grime of our unbelief, our blatant sin, or our disobedience? We can barely look at ourselves without cringing; how could He truly see us and want to stay near?

These black lies linger, but a white blaze of light shines into our hearts, and suddenly we are filled with a warmth and hope we didn't dare dream possible. The God of the universe calls to us and reminds us of who He is and how He loves.

> Where shall I go from your Spirit?
> Or where shall I flee from your presence?
> If I ascend to heaven, you are there!
> If I make my bed in Sheol, you are there!
> If I take the wings of the morning
> and dwell in the uttermost parts of the sea,
> even there your hand shall lead me,
> and your right hand shall hold me.
> If I say, "Surely the darkness shall cover me,
> and the light about me be night,"
> even the darkness is not dark to you;
> the night is bright as the day,
> for darkness is as light with you. (Psalm 139:7–12 ESV)

In the dark waters of the womb, God fashioned and formed us, saw who we were and who we'd become. He knows us well. He is not afraid to travel to the depths and unearth the grime of our sin, nor is He hesitant to trek our unstable terrain to take our burdens from our heaving hearts.

There is nowhere we can go where He is not already. His presence promises peace and light, for even the darkness is not dark to Him. And because of Jesus Christ's death and resurrection, our own lives are resurrected out of the dark and into His wondrous light.

Step out of the shadows. God knows you, God sees you, and His love is waiting. We can leave our shame at the foot of the cross. Let His light flood in and find a home in your heart today.

JOURNAL PROMPT

Share with God what is on your heart. Invite Him to light the dark spaces of your life and fill you with His love.

___

___

___

___

___

___

___

___

___

___

___

___

23

Will Morning Ever Come?

ALICIA BRUXVOORT

He is here: the one who forms the mountains, creates the wind, and reveals his thoughts to man, the one who makes the dawn out of darkness and strides on the heights of the earth. The LORD, the God of Armies, is his name.

AMOS 4:13

I heard the pitter-patter of his feet before his voice woke me on that night long ago. "Is it morning yet?" The shaft of moonlight on the floor confirmed I didn't need to glance at the clock to answer his question.

"No, buddy," I murmured as I gently steered him back to bed.

When his little body wouldn't surrender to sleep, he slipped out of the bottom bunk and pressed his nose to the window. There, he watched and waited for daybreak.

The hours stretched long, and his patience wore thin, so he woke me again with a worried whimper. "Mommy, will morning *ever* come?" Empathy welled in my weariness. After all, little boys aren't the only ones who pose anxious questions in the dark.

When I'm stuck in the shadows of uncertainty or the gloom of grief, the eclipse of apprehension or the fog of fear, I often wonder the same thing:

Will peace ever prevail over this pain?
Will joy ever replace this sadness?
Will beauty ever grow from this brokenness?
Will morning ever come?

Thankfully, Amos 4:13 reminds us we're not alone when our hope grows dim:

> He is here: the one who forms the mountains, creates the wind, and reveals his thoughts to man, the one who makes the dawn out of darkness and strides on the heights of the earth. The LORD, the God of Armies, is his name.

While I'm comforted by the assurance of God's power and presence, my favorite part of this verse is tucked between the description of His majesty and His might: "The one who makes the dawn out of darkness."

The original word for *makes* carries the idea of fashioning or producing with intention and commitment. Amazingly, the same God who shaped the mountains and crafted the wind is not only *capable* of bringing the light of His hope into the depths of our darkness but *committed* to it.

Thanks to that unchanging truth, we can put our confidence in God's follow-through even before we see the fruit of His faithfulness. Of course, Amos 4:13 doesn't just boost our confidence in shadowy seasons; it buoys our patience too.

The poignant imagery of dawn emphasizes a truth I'm prone to forget:

Hope doesn't always arrive like a spotlight. Sometimes it simply shows up like a sunrise. Just as daybreak unfolds with steady streaks and gentle gleams, so God works all things for our good and His glory, one flicker of faithfulness at a time.

That's why, on that night long ago, I walked my son back to his window and pointed out a faint glow on the horizon.

"See that?" I asked as I wrapped my arms around his slender frame. "God is making the morning, just like He always does."

And together, we watched dawn rise from darkness, one silent shimmer at a time.

JOURNAL PROMPT

How have you seen God's flickers of faithfulness lately?

_____

_____

_____

_____

_____

_____

_____

_____

_____

24

When You Feel Lost, Jesus Is the Way

ASHLEY MORGAN JACKSON

I am the Lord. I have called you for a righteous purpose, and I will hold you by your hand. I will watch over you, and I will appoint you to be a covenant for the people and a light to the nations, in order to open blind eyes, to bring out prisoners from the dungeon, and those sitting in darkness from the prison house.

ISAIAH 42:6–7

I had lost him. He was three years old and had been playing on the playground just behind me as I sat on a picnic bench waiting for my other son to meet me at the elementary school blacktop. As a sea of kids streamed out of their classrooms and I searched for my older son, I looked back to check on my youngest and couldn't see him anywhere.

The panic slowly rose as I checked all the spots where he normally played. I started to let the other parents around know to look and was screaming his name. He was lost, and he needed me. Not a moment later, a man who always walked his daughters to school with us arrived, my toddler in hand. I thanked him profusely and hugged my son tightly.

My son hadn't meant to, but he had gotten mixed in with the crowd and lost sight of me.

Have you ever lost sight of how you got here or which direction you needed to go? It is so scary to be lost, not to be able to see the way and not to know what to do next.

We never intend to get lost. Maybe we got swept up with the crowd, depended on ourselves more than we should have, or were shaken because life felt unknown and dark. Sometimes even when we are sure we've chosen the right way, over time we lose sight of our Father, the one who guides and protects us.

Oh, friend, the Lord knew we would need a light to guide us back to His loving arms. Isaiah 42:6–7 prophesied of the coming Messiah, Jesus, saying,

> I am the LORD. I have called you for a righteous purpose, and I will hold you by your hand. I will watch over you, and I will appoint you to be a covenant for the people and a light to the nations, in order to open blind eyes, to bring out prisoners from the dungeon, and those sitting in darkness from the prison house.

This was Jesus' mission. He was sent by God to provide a light for our dark path when we are lost so that we might find our way back to the Father. Jesus came to open our eyes, to set us free when we are trapped, and to illuminate our path when things have become impossibly dim.

Jesus came for us; we don't have to live lost. When we don't know the way, we can always look to Him in His Word. He will never fail to shine a light on the path that leads us back to safety.

JOURNAL PROMPT

In what areas of your life have you felt lost, unsure, or stuck? What have these things caused you to do, think, or feel? How might applying the light of Jesus to these circumstances help you?

25

The Game God Will Deliver You

MEREDITH HOUSTON CARR

I will lead the blind by a way they did not know; I will guide them on paths they have not known. I will turn darkness to light in front of them and rough places into level ground. This is what I will do for them, and I will not abandon them.

ISAIAH 42:16

On a bright, balmy day several springs ago, I received one of *those* phone calls that leave you speechless, stunned, and spinning.

As gently as she could, my son's doctor not only confirmed his autism diagnosis but also added a second bit of shocking news: Additional testing revealed he had a rare genetic anomaly.

The "cherry on top" of the bad news sundae, if you will.

Streams of bold California sunshine streaked through the window and fell on my face, but at that moment, my entire world plunged into darkness.

How were we going to find our way through this? How would we locate the help our son needed? And how would we figure out *what* help he needed in the first place?

There was no manual, no guide, and what felt like no hope. Despair settled into my soul and turned me into a shell of the woman I was before. Because that's what happens when we enter a dark season, isn't it? Hope goes out the window, and we wonder how God's light could ever get in *here*.

Here, amid divorce or health crises. Financial disasters or family dysfunctions. Pain, shame, or blame. In our most dismal moments, we might wonder if God is helpless to rescue us, or worse—has He abandoned us altogether?

You're not alone if you are walking in the shadow of despair. Centuries ago, God's chosen people, the southern kingdom of Judah, walked through a dark season of captivity and desolation. God sent the prophet Isaiah to deliver spirit-bolstering words, and these words can strengthen our modern-day spirits too.

I invite you to quiet your mind for a moment and let today's key verse settle over you:

> I will lead the blind by a way they did not know; I will guide them on paths they have not known. I will turn darkness to light in front of them and rough places into level ground. This is what I will do for them, and I will not abandon them. (Isaiah 42:16)

With vivid word pictures, Isaiah reminded us that God's deliverance is *sure*—our blindness, confusion, and rocky roads can't stop the Father's light from seeping in where we need it most.

The future may appear uncertain to us, but it's not uncertain to our Guide. Indeed, all our fears of abandonment or helplessness melt in the face of His promise to move us forward, even when we see no way through.

You don't have to walk in despair when hardship darkens your path because *God has promised to lead you out.* You don't have to lead yourself! Your loving Father will illuminate every dark corner and flatten every rock blocking your way.

The same God who delivered Judah from all its troubles will deliver you too.

I've navigated special-needs parenting for a decade now, and I stand amazed at God's guidance through all the confusion, doubt, and fear. He has been faithful to His promises.

He longs to do the same for you, dear one. May the truth of His Word and the certainty of His guidance strengthen our spirits for the days ahead.

JOURNAL PROMPT

Take some time to reflect on a dark or difficult road you've walked. As you look back, write down all the ways, big and small, you can see God's good hand guiding you. Then take time to write about how this evidence can strengthen you and fill you with hope for your current or future trials.

26

We Are Chosen to Shine Light in the Darkness

DORINA LAZO GILMORE-YOUNG

But you are a chosen race, a royal priesthood, a holy nation, a people for his possession, so that you may proclaim the praises of the one who called you out of darkness into his marvelous light.

I PETER 2:9

When one of my daughters tried out for a local club soccer team, she was among the youngest of the girls at tryouts. She also had fewer years of experience compared to many of the girls who had been playing longer. We were surprised when she got a callback and was eventually chosen for the team.

In God's economy, being chosen does not depend on our age, experience, or position in society. He chooses us in spite of our sin and shortcomings. He pulls us from darkness into light to be on His team.

In Peter's letter to the believers scattered throughout Asia Minor, he wrote, "But you are a chosen race, a royal priesthood, a holy nation, a people for his possession, so that you may proclaim the praises of the one who called you out of darkness into his marvelous light" (1 Peter 2:9).

Peter was writing from Rome to remind discouraged believers that they were a "chosen race." The dictionary says someone who is *chosen* is "the object of divine favor." Throughout the pages of Scripture, this word is used to mean "examined, preferred, and selected."

We were chosen to be distinct, spiritual, and physical beings, reflecting God's glory to the world. Peter reminded us that we were once living in darkness, but Jesus chose us for His team and called us out into His marvelous light—the light of salvation. Jesus chose to die a horrible death on the cross so we might live in eternity with our heavenly Father. God's Son, Jesus, was His rescue plan for us in the darkness.

Friend, you and I are chosen by God, not by our own merit but because of His grace. We are chosen to bring light to who He is and how He is working. We are chosen to be lanterns of hope in times of grief and uncertainty. We are called to illuminate the story of His faithfulness to a weary world.

When your days feel dark or uncertain, hang on to the truth and the hope that *you are God's chosen one.* His light will still shine through you and for you, no matter what you are facing.

JOURNAL PROMPT

Can you think of a time when you were chosen for something and it made you feel special or singled out? Now that you've been chosen for God's team, how can you invite others into His marvelous light?

_____

_____

_____

_____

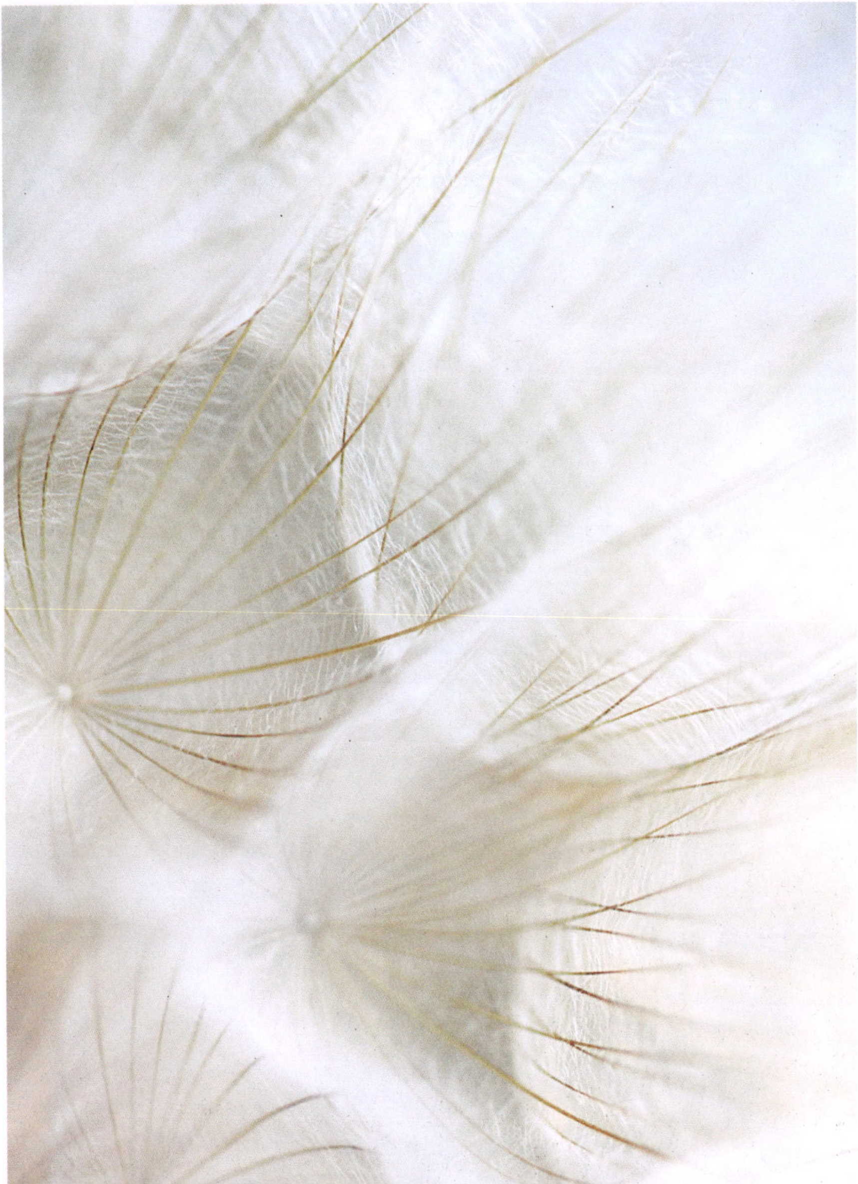

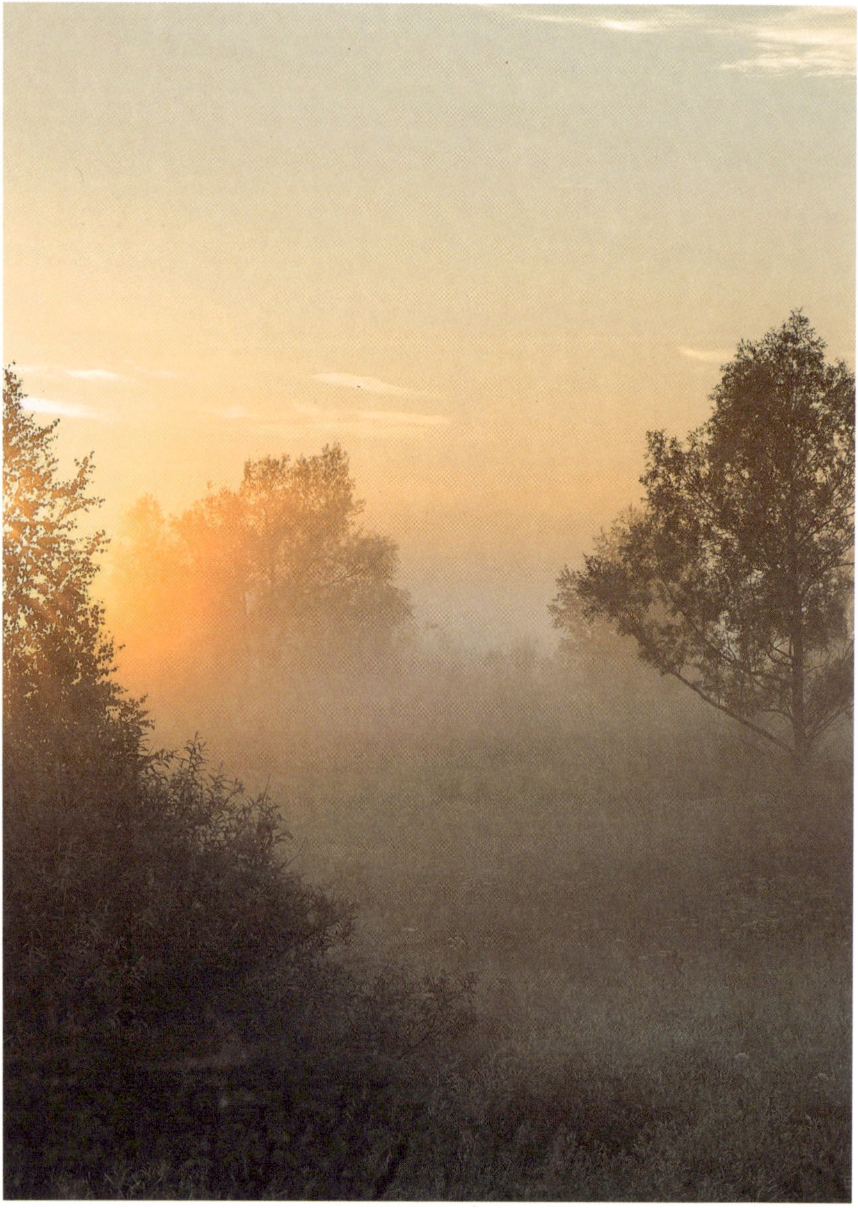

PART 6

A New Dawn Is Coming

Shadows are evidence that light exists. We know light is there, but sometimes it's partially covered. Scripture tells us the Old Testament laws were a shadow of something greater to come: Jesus, our Messiah, who fulfilled the law through His sinless life and sacrificial death. The dawn was coming!

27

The Treasure of Night Faith

DR. ALICIA BRITT CHOLE

I will give you the treasures of darkness and riches from secret places, so that you may know that I am the LORD. I am the God of Israel, who calls you by your name.

ISAIAH 45:3

In hindsight, it was unwise to sit alone in that forgotten, unkempt park. But sit I did, head in hands, unconsciously rocking, desperately trying to make my faith stay put, stay whole, simply . . . stay.

The picnic bench on which I was perched looked like my faith felt: weathered, unstable, and beyond repair.

> There was no blood.
> There had been no documentable tragedy.
> The battle within, however, had been brutal.

I was struggling with the character—with the very nature—of God.

How on earth did I get here? I winced.

"Here" was a space that faithful followers of God have referred to for centuries as "the night"—seasons in which (spiritually speaking) we can't see straight and we don't feel great. Without a theological framework for such seasons, our tendency is to assume that entering a night means we're exiting the faith.

No. It's just a night. And the night was one of the original residents of Eden.

> And [God] separated the light from the darkness. God called the light "day," and the darkness he called "night." ... God made two great lights—the greater light to govern the day and the lesser light to govern the night.... And God saw that it was good. (Genesis 1:4-5, 16, 18 NIV)

In the creation story, day complemented (as opposed to voided) the night. Pre-sin, pre-fall, pre-curse, and pre-drama, walking with God has always required both day faith and night faith.

Physically, we have a rather long history of efforts to eliminate or at least shorten the night. With candles or clicks, every age has tried to make the night bow to its perceived need for more light and less darkness.

Thankfully, we are slowly regaining respect for night's healing powers as researchers affirm the clear connection between darkness, sleep, immune system health, and mental and emotional wellness.

Even so, we still are reticent to respect the night spiritually.

We prefer to grow by day, thank you. We prefer faith in full sun. We prefer to see clearly, to feel fully, and to walk confidently into a well-lit future.

But what if spiritual nights are essential? What if there is something we need in the night that cannot be found in the day?

This was definitely part of my struggle on that park bench. I was desperately trying to climb out of the night because I perceived it as failure, especially in contrast to what I had experienced up to that point.

In hindsight, I realized that God was inviting me into night faith. And though I never could have anticipated it, night faith would soon lead me into something far more satisfying than understanding and far more powerful than peace: a purified devotion to God.

Like the night I was in the middle of on that old park bench, your night will not last forever. But within it is a treasure that's simply too weighty to be held by sunshine.

<small>Adapted from Alicia Britt Chole, *The Night Is Normal: A Guide Through Spiritual Pain*, (Tyndale House Publishers, 2023). Used by permission of Tyndale House Publishers.</small>

JOURNAL PROMPT

Though we want to avoid the hard places in life, we will inevitably spend time there. The good news is that God wastes nothing. What treasures have you discovered in the "night" seasons of your life?

_____

_____

_____

_____

_____

_____

28

No Longer Afraid of the Dark

MEREDITH HOUSTON CARR

The people walking in darkness have seen a great light;
a light has dawned on those living in the land of darkness.

ISAIAH 9:2

When my children were little, they experienced what so many young ones do—a palpable, potent fear of the dark. No matter how much encouragement I offered, the only thing powerful enough to alleviate their fear was a night-light (preferably in the shape of a favorite cartoon character).

I can chuckle at the memory now, but a deep sigh bubbles up as I realize that *you and I aren't so different from children*. Even as adults, we can still be afraid of the dark. Especially the darkness of the unknown as we navigate complicated relationships, broken dreams, crushed expectations, and difficult trials that often leave us on edge, waiting for the other shoe to drop.

Yes, we fear the dark, when these things and a thousand more overshadow our path. We run from it or ignore it. We seek a night-light because we don't know how to sit with the dark, either in our lives or the lives of others.

During my darkest days as the mom of a special-needs child, I remember the well-meaning people who tried to alleviate my fears by putting a bright spin on our circumstances. I appreciated their efforts, but it didn't help because there was no way around it—our season *was* dark.

Maybe you're in a shadowy season today. If so, you are not alone. God's Word catalogs many stories of faithful followers who have traversed the valley just like you and me. Even God's beloved nation of Judah experienced a prolonged, oppressive season. They couldn't see a way through—but *we* know the beautiful truth that God never intended to leave them in the dark.

And He doesn't intend to leave you in darkness either. The prophet Isaiah lit the way to hope by helping Judah—and us—remember that God was planning to usher in a brand-new chapter:

> The people walking in darkness have seen a great light; a light has dawned on those living in the land of darkness. (Isaiah 9:2)

On this side of history, we have the advantage of knowing that the light of *Jesus* was coming. And with Him came all the truth and grace we need to live victoriously in the dark. So no matter how vigorously our Enemy works to keep us stuck in darkness, Jesus—our Savior, God *with us*—is working out His greater agenda.

His agenda includes turning darkness into light, loss into abundance, and despair into joy. Indeed, He's so much more than a night-light!

Dear one, whatever darkness overshadows your path, you don't have to deny it, minimize it, or pretend it doesn't exist. You also don't have to fear it. As it was for the people of Judah, darkness may be a *part* of your story today, but it's not the *whole* story.

The light of Jesus is coming for you.

JOURNAL PROMPT

Have you ever been in a situation where well-meaning people tried to "shine a light," so to speak, on your situation but in a way that was not honoring or acknowledging the hard situation? How can we shine differently for those who are suffering? Is there someone in your life who needs to feel seen right now?

29

Hope in the Darkness

STACY J. LOWE

Weeping may stay overnight, but there is joy in the morning.
PSALM 30:5

I'm not a big fan of darkness, though I don't really know who is. When nighttime closes in, like many, I head indoors, shut the blinds, and flip a switch to once again surround myself with light.

This strategy works well for literal darkness, but what about a darkness of the soul? When everything around you feels wrong and out of place? When you want nothing more than to see and feel the sunshine once again? Can the flip of a switch solve *that*?

I wish it could. And we *do* try. We'll sometimes fill the void around us with other things (nonstop activity or binge-watching our favorite shows) in an attempt to distract ourselves from what's really happening. But in the end, that's *all* it is—a *distraction*. What we really need in times of darkness is a spot of hope to fix our eyes upon.

This was something King David understood well, and from a place of firsthand experience, he penned these words:

> Weeping may stay overnight, but there is joy in the morning. (Psalm 30:5)

You see, David knew a thing or two about darkness. He knew what it was like to be overlooked by others. To be the underdog. To lose a best friend. To be on the run in fear for his life. But he also knew how God always showed up for him, even in the darkest of times. In fact, many of the psalms written by David are his boasting of all the things the Lord had done. Recounting God's past goodness toward him seems to have infused David with a confidence to boldly proclaim the joy he knew was to come.

Do you share that same confidence? In the midst of your tears, do you, too, know the light is coming? Because it is.

Our God has not forgotten us, and He has not left us on our own. Even when we can't feel His presence, He is still right there beside us—always—no matter how dark the night. Sometimes we need to remind ourselves of that and, like David, recall His track record of faithfulness toward us. Not just call it to mind, either, but *declare* it to ourselves as a predictor of what's to come.

Doing so is like a pep talk to the soul, pointing us to hope, pointing us to the horizon where the sun's rays will soon peek over once again.

We *will* walk through seasons of grief and struggle. There's just no getting around that. But we get to choose how we'll spend that time. We can distract ourselves and try to numb the pain, or we can fix our eyes on hope and remember the night won't last forever.

In my own time of weeping, I choose to recall God's goodness and remind myself that morning is on the way. *Joy* is on the way. I choose to watch the horizon so as not to miss the first glimpse of the coming light. Will you do the same?

JOURNAL PROMPT

How has God shown up for you in the past? What can you point to in your life and say, "I *know* that was God"? Begin a list of these God-moments and read them back to yourself as a reminder of the joy that's to come.

_____

_____

_____

_____

_____

_____

_____

_____

_____

_____

_____

_____

30

I See Your Father in You

ELIZABETH LAING THOMPSON

Long ago God spoke to our ancestors by the prophets at different times and in different ways. In these last days, he has spoken to us by his Son. God has appointed him heir of all things and made the universe through him. The Son is the radiance of God's glory and the exact expression of his nature, sustaining all things by his powerful word.

HEBREWS 1:1–3

"You remind me of your dad."

A smiling woman approached me, speaking over the joyful hubbub of church fellowship. "I was a member of a congregation he pastored years ago, and I see your father in you."

I tucked the woman's words into my heart like precious treasure—*You remind me of your dad. I see your father in you*—because my dad is my hero and I can think of no greater compliment.

Two thousand years ago, a Son named Jesus came to earth to reflect His Father. The writer of Hebrews told us,

> Long ago God spoke to our ancestors by the prophets at different times and in different ways. In these last days, he has spoken to us by his Son. God has appointed him heir of all things and made the universe through him. The Son is the radiance of God's glory and the exact expression of his nature, sustaining all things by his powerful word. (Hebrews 1:1–3)

Jesus not only sustains all creation, but He radiates God's glory and expresses His nature. Just as a lamp reflected in a mirror shines doubly bright, so Jesus mirrors and magnifies God's nature. When we long to see God, we can look to His Son.

Jesus spoke often about this. After raising Lazarus from the dead, He cried, "The one who sees me sees him who sent me. I have come as light into the world, so that everyone who believes in me would not remain in darkness" (John 12:45–46). Before He went to the cross, Jesus told His disciples, "The one who has seen me has seen the Father" (14:9).

God sent Jesus to reflect His light and character so we could better understand God Himself. It's as though God thought to Himself, *I don't think My children understand who I am and how I love. They need to see to understand.*

And so God took His life-sparking, star-spinning power, compressed it into DNA, and wrapped it in fragile human skin. He took His wide-as-the-universe love off heaven's throne and sent it to walk, sandal-clad, down dusty streets, side by side with the lost and lonely. With this astounding move, it's as if God was saying, "Don't just take My word for it—let Me show you how I love."

As Jesus walked this planet, He gave Scripture skin and bone; He turned lofty, divine promises into tender moments of conversation and connection.

It's one thing to read, "The Lord is a compassionate and gracious God" (Exodus 34:6), but through Jesus' life, we see God's compassion in action. We watch His healing hand reach out to do the unthinkable, the forbidden: He touched a leper, an outcast who probably hadn't felt the warmth of human touch since the day he fell ill (Luke 5:12–13).

It's one thing to read, "The Lord is . . . slow to anger" (Exodus 34:6), but through Jesus' friendships, we see God's patience. We watch Jesus remind His competitive disciples (yet again) that leadership isn't about power and position; it's about sacrificial service (Matthew 20:20–28).

It's one thing to read, "He forgives all your iniquity" (Psalm 103:3), but through Jesus' death, we see God's forgiveness—and how much it cost. We watch Jesus, nailed to a tree and struggling to breathe, yet pushing grace past His pain: "Father, forgive them" (Luke 23:34).

The dazzling light of God's love blazes forth from Jesus' life:

Welcoming the lonely.

Bearing with the weak.

Forgiving the unworthy.

Reflecting the Father's glory.

And when we see Jesus, our hearts can't help but say, *You remind me of Your Dad. I see your Father in You.*

JOURNAL PROMPT

What quality of Jesus helps you better understand your heavenly Father? How do you hope people see your Father in you?

_____

_____

_____

_____

_____

_____

_____

_____

31

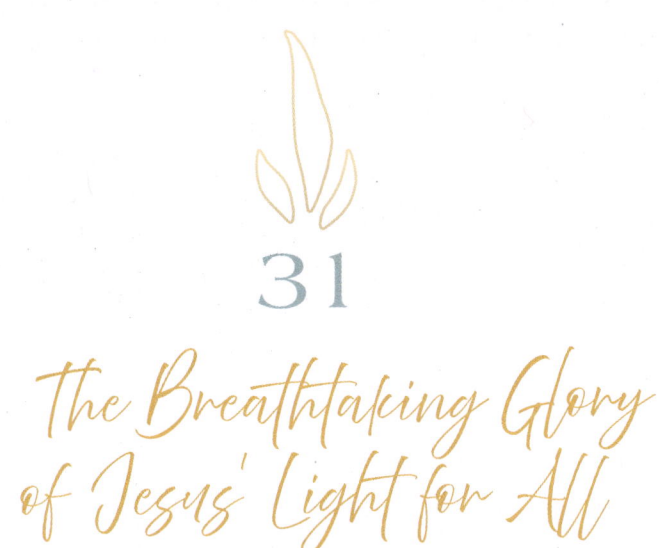

The Breathtaking Glory of Jesus' Light for All

ASHERITAH CIUCIU

The true light that gives light to everyone
was coming into the world.

JOHN 1:9

Has a sunset ever taken your breath away?

The rays of light disperse into the atmosphere with a brilliant display of colors that shift from one minute to the next. No matter how many sunsets I've witnessed, each iridescent show interrupts my agenda with the wonder of the glory of God.

It baffles me that God offers this radiant gift to everyone—yet only those who pause to look up and observe it actually receive it. Everyone else continues their busy lives as if a cosmic art show wasn't happening in the sky above.

The Bible tells us that when Jesus came to earth, His radiant glory shone for all to see—but only those with eyes of faith perceived and received: "The true light that gives light to everyone was coming into the world" (John 1:9). Here we find an understated truth too marvelous for comprehension: The One who commanded "Let there be light" on the dawn of creation entered the created world (Genesis 1:3). The One who spoke the sun and stars into existence now offers Himself as true light within us.

God Himself, Light eternal, placed within human hearts. Oh, how glorious!

And Jesus' generosity knows no bounds. Just as "He causes his sun to rise on the evil and the good," so He offers His true light to *everyone* who believes (Matthew 5:45 NIV). Jesus could have easily limited His lavish offer only to the Jews or only to the religious elite or only to those who lived in His generation. But instead, He offers Himself to *everyone*. We need only *look* with eyes of faith to receive Jesus' eternal illumination that shines brightly in every generation.

Sadly, not everyone receives His light. Just as some people ignore sunsets, there are those who ignore the true Light of the World, to their eternal loss.

But this is also true: Just as every sunrise brings a new day with fresh opportunities, so every moment we draw breath is a new invitation to come and behold the beauty of Jesus. As long as you breathe, it's never too late to receive His light.

And just as one person pausing to stare at the sunset will draw others to behold its beauty, so also when we look to Jesus, our faces will radiate His glory, causing others to pause and look to Him too.

JOURNAL PROMPT

Pause at some point today or in the next few days, and behold God's glory in the natural world. Then record what you saw and learned about God.

32

Shadows Prove the Light

ERIC GAGNON

*Since the law has only a shadow of the good things to come,
and not the reality itself of those things, it can
never perfect the worshipers by the same sacrifices
they continually offer year after year.*

HEBREWS 10:1

When my son was little, we played with a flashlight in the dark at bedtime. I would position my hand and the flashlight so all we could see was a small shadow of my hand growing larger until it looked like it could carry us away. We laughed together at the wonder of how a shadow looked so much like a giant hand coming to get us. It was fun because we knew what created the shadow.

But imagine if we didn't know. That would change things quite a bit for us. When we don't know what causes a shadow, it can make us confused, fearful even.

God's Word in Hebrews 10:1 compares a "shadow" to the parts of the Old Testament that used to be confusing and even scary. God's light has always been shining in the pages of His Word, but people didn't always see exactly how He planned to save us from sin and death. The ceremonial laws and the temple sacrifices seemed to promise hope but never quite delivered.

Then Jesus came. The mystery was revealed. Being fully God and fully man, Jesus gave His life once for all as a payment for sin for all who turn to and trust Him for salvation.

> For by one offering he has perfected forever those who are sanctified. (Hebrews 10:14)

Many of us are familiar with this truth, but what we don't often stop to think about is that just as the Old Testament clearly foreshadowed the coming of Christ, the very presence of the church today in the world foreshadows His second coming. As sure as we can look around and see evidence that Jesus was here, we can also know He is coming again soon.

And very soon, every shadowy place will disappear because we know the Light has come and the Light will come again.

Like my son and me with the flashlight in his bedroom, we can have understanding and no fear as we read God's Word together today, even the Old Testament, because we know who the Light is and we know and trust His hand, even in the shadowy places.

JOURNAL PROMPT

Are there any parts of the Bible you find particularly hard to read or difficult to understand? How can you see the light of Jesus in those areas?

_____

_____

_____

_____

_____

_____

_____

_____

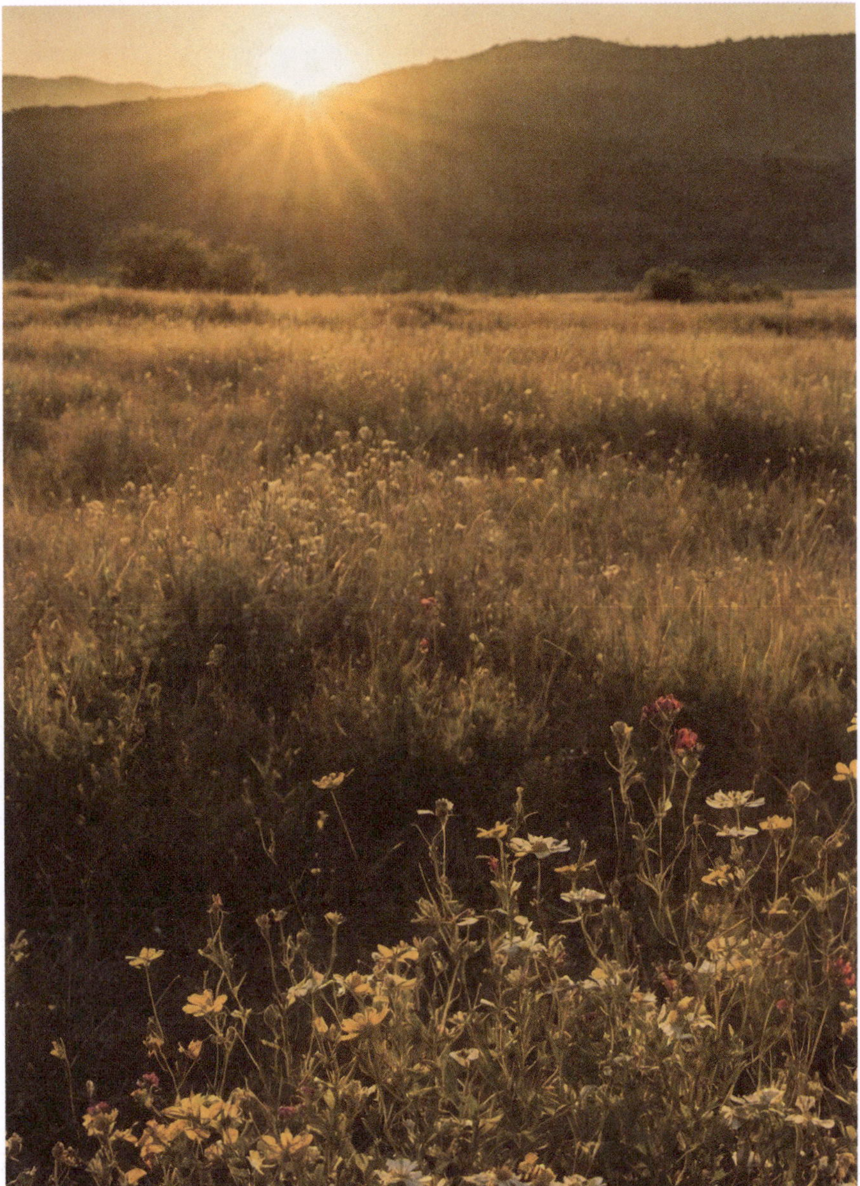

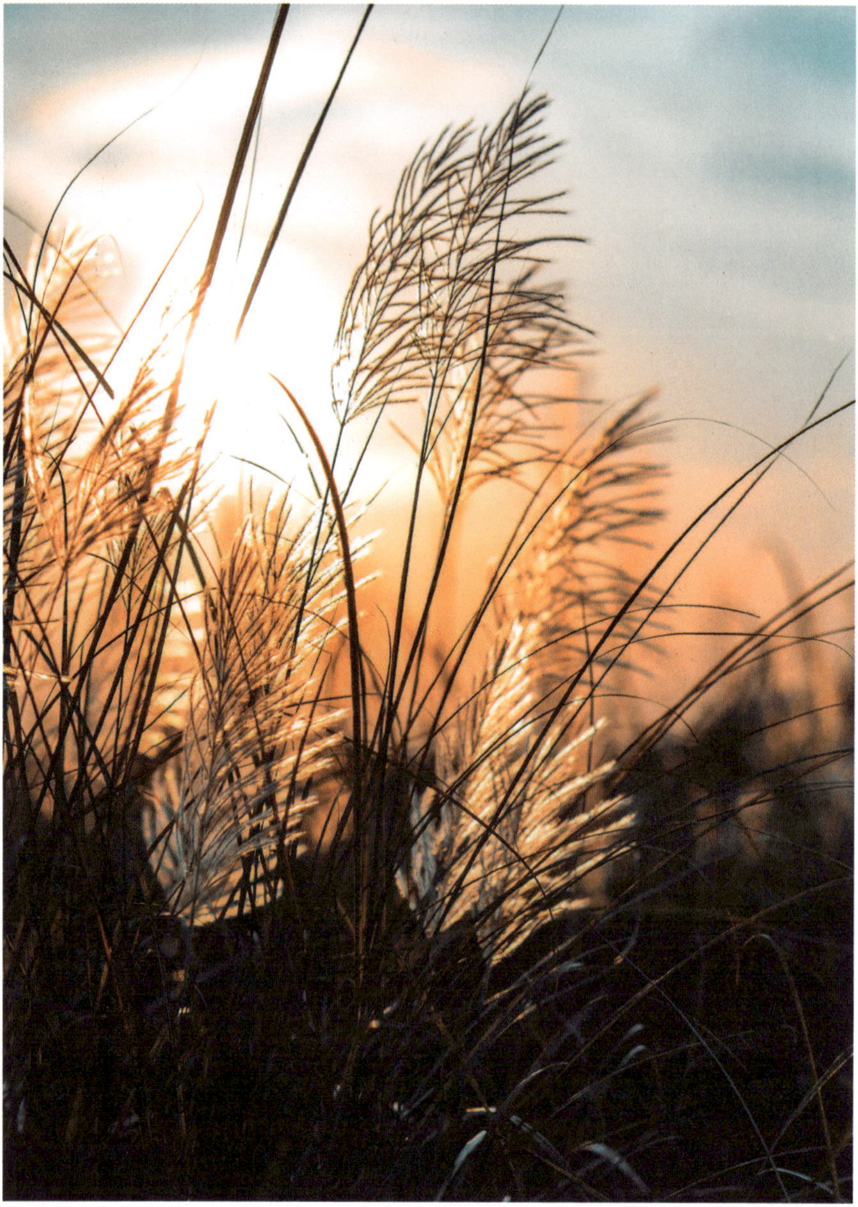

PART 7

Jesus Is the Light of the World

To a world plunged in spiritual darkness, Jesus is the light. To the lost, He is the way. To the hurting, He is healing. To all in sin, He is salvation. Jesus is God's plan to redeem and restore all people to Himself. It's His pattern to reveal Himself in light, and Jesus is the light of God's redemption and the promise of life everlasting.

33

Message of the Magi

MEGHAN MELLINGER

Where is he who has been born king of the Jews? For we saw his star at its rising and have come to worship him.

MATTHEW 2:2

It was a clear and calm night. The usual stars assumed their usual spots in the black canvas of the sky. Until a newcomer appeared and stole the celestial show.

Years of studying the skies confirmed, this wasn't just any new star.

This was *the* star.

The star for *the* King.

So the wise men, or magi, journeyed to Jerusalem to ask the king of the country where they could find the King of all kings: "Where is he who has been born king of the Jews? For we saw his star at its rising and have come to worship him" (Matthew 2:2).

Their inquiry led them to Bethlehem, but it was the star that led them to the infant Jesus:

> And there it was—the star they had seen at its rising. It led them until it came and stopped above the place where the child was. (Matthew 2:9)

This wasn't just any new star.
This star was supernatural.
This star *moved*.
Was it a shooting star or comet, a supernova, or a conjunction of planets?
Whatever the astronomical phenomenon was, it was a divine guide right to the cradle of the newborn King. When the wise men came face-to-face with the King of the Jews, they fell down in worship, offering fine gifts fitting only for royalty.

But the message of the magi here is more than a Christmas card picture of a star and three regal silhouettes on camelback. The message of the magi is about a loving and relational God meeting us right where we are.

The wise men were a pagan people. They studied stars, not Scripture. So God spoke to them in a language they would understand: the skies.

God met the men living in darkness right where they were by capturing their upward gaze with a mysterious light. He used their sense of wonder for the stars to bring them face-to-face with the wonder of their Savior. And they were filled with joy and awe, falling to their knees in worship. What they had thought was magical was nothing in light of a personal experience with the Light of the World.

God illuminated the skies to illuminate the magi's hearts—and ours.

The God of the universe humbled Himself in the form of a child to meet us exactly where we are: in our sin on earth. Divinity dwelling in human form, with us, beside us, for us. And ultimately dying to save us.

This wasn't just any new star.

This was a star for the King, our Savior—who takes us by the hand and leads us out of darkness. The light in the sky proclaimed the best news we'll ever hear: The Light of the World is with us, beside us, for us. Walking alongside us. Speaking to us in a language we'll hear and can't help but respond to with hearts full of awe and wonder and worship.

JOURNAL PROMPT

While you probably don't have any myrrh in your cupboard, what gift can you bring in awe and wonder today to our Savior, who is meeting you right where you are?

_____

_____

_____

_____

_____

_____

_____

_____

_____

_____

34

A Spectacular Light for Everyone

DORINA LAZO GILMORE-YOUNG

For my eyes have seen your salvation. You have prepared it in the presence of all peoples—a light for revelation to the Gentiles and glory to your people Israel.

LUKE 2:30–32

Have you ever been outside the city and looked up to see a sky full of stars?

The first time I visited the northern mountains of Haiti for a mission trip, a group of us went outside after dark and saw the most spectacular light show of stars. As our eyes adjusted to the dark, we could see more and more stars.

We looked up with a hushed sense of awe and wonder as we witnessed God's glorious creation. The North Star shone the brightest of them all. It reminded me of what Simeon said about our true light, Jesus.

Tucked in the Gospel of Luke, chapter 2, is the story of Mary and Joseph bringing the young Jesus to the temple in Jerusalem. At the temple, they met a faithful man named Simeon, who was guided by the Holy Spirit and had waited many years with hope of seeing the Messiah before he died.

When Simeon took young Jesus into his arms, he said, "My eyes have seen your salvation. You have prepared it in the presence of all peoples—a light for revelation to the Gentiles and glory to your people Israel" (Luke 2:30–32).

In his declaration, Simeon referenced the words of the prophet Isaiah, which describe the Messiah as being "a light to the nations" (Isaiah 42:6). Jesus is the fulfillment of God's promises and prophecy for the people of Israel (the Jews) and the plan of salvation for Gentiles (which includes any of us who believe).

When Simeon held Jesus up, he was calling out the dual nature of Jesus' mission on earth—to bring glory to Israel and the light of truth to the nations. God spoke through Simeon and prophesied that His salvation was universal. He was making it known that Jesus was God's plan to unite the world to Himself.

When I was in Haiti staring up at the star-studded sky, I realized that though I was thousands of miles away from my family in the United States, the very same stars that illuminated the sky in Haiti also brightened the sky for them. The very same North Star shone for them too—just like Jesus, the Light of the World.

Next time you go outside at night—wherever you are in the world—think about how Jesus is our guiding North Star, pointing people back to the grace and mercy of the Creator, our heavenly Father.

JOURNAL PROMPT

Where have you witnessed the most amazing starlight show, and how does that view remind you of Jesus?

35

Dawn of Grace

BRENDA BRADFORD OTTINGER

I have come as light into the world, so that everyone who believes in me would not remain in darkness.

JOHN 12:46

For as long as I can remember, my eyes have been drawn to the sky, forever gazing into the wonder draped across the canvas above: bowed promise after the rain, glory aflame as the sun melts to sleep, glitter aglow in the night. But it's the sunrise that has my heart with its radiant hope lighting up the dark as the lantern in the sky births another day.

How fitting that Jesus—the Lamb of God who humbly moved into this world to save it—is described as "light" in Scripture. In some of His last earthly words, Jesus told the crowds gathered around Him, "I have come as light into the world, so that everyone who believes in me would not remain in darkness" (John 12:46).

Hundreds of years before, the prophet Malachi foretold that the Messiah would come as the "sun of righteousness" (Malachi 4:2), and then Jesus, the Light of the World, stood in their midst. The dawn of the new covenant of grace had arrived to redeem a world of hearts to God.

And, oh, how Jesus longed for His cherished people to believe *He* was their way of salvation, having declared, "I am the way, the truth, and the life. No one comes to the Father except through me" (John 14:6).

Jesus is not only a light on earth now, but the book of Revelation tells us that one day, when everything is made new, the city of God will "not need the sun or the moon to shine on it, because the glory of God illuminates it, and its lamp is the Lamb" (Revelation 21:23).

Dear friend, the Lamp of Heaven became the Light of the World, stepping across the threshold of humanity to garner grace for us with His precious life! And that grace does not expire. No darkness of this world has the power to overshadow His eternal light, for even today His grace envelops us. Belief in Jesus Christ as Lord is *our* way to life with God.

Not only does Jesus save us into eternal life with God, but every day He saves us from the folly of our humanity. These human hearts of ours can stray, but greater is the God within us than the Evil One of the world.

Take heart, friend, for even when we slip and stumble in the dark, as we return to His Word and walk in the light of His example, His grace forever flows.

Oh, that the Son would have our hearts and we'd gaze into the wonder of His ways as we seek to live *in* this world and not be *of* it. For the dawn of redemption rises in our midst each day, birthing new mercies and fresh strength as His radiant grace drapes across the canvas of our lives.

JOURNAL PROMPT

Write a prayer of gratitude and commitment to Jesus, centering your life in His light.

_____

_____

_____

_____

_____

_____

_____

_____

36

Stick Close to the Light

ALICIA BRUXVOORT

Jesus spoke to them again: "I am the light of the world. Anyone who follows me will never walk in the darkness but will have the light of life."

JOHN 8:12

When I announced we were trading our bedtime story for a real-time adventure, eight little girls danced around me with wide-eyed expectancy.

"We're going on a night hike," I said as we stepped into the velvety darkness on the last night of summer camp. I waved a flashlight above my head and gave my treasured troupe one simple instruction: "The path through the woods is dark, so stick close and follow me."

Most of the girls heeded my words without question and followed the flashlight's gentle gleam. But as we rounded a brambly bend, we heard a yelp of distress behind us. When we tracked the sound to its source, we found a wayward camper sitting on the ground with a swollen lip and bleeding knee.

"I wanted to find a shortcut," she exclaimed when I asked why she'd wandered so far from the trail. "But I got confused in the dark and tripped on that giant stump." She pointed to what remained of a rotting tree and began to cry.

I pulled her into my arms and murmured words of comfort, but her best friend stated the obvious: "That's why you should've stuck by the light!"

I've never roamed the darkened woods alone, but I've tried to forge my way across the dust of this broken world. And when I rely on my limited wisdom and shadowy vision to navigate life's challenges, I end up disoriented and discouraged like that little girl.

Thankfully, we don't have to walk alone. John 8:12 reminds us Jesus is willing to pilot our path: "I am the light of the world. Anyone who follows me will never walk in the darkness but will have the light of life."

I love the promise of a Savior who will illuminate my steps. But as my wandering camper discovered, a guiding light is useless if we're not close enough to see it. Perhaps that's why, after announcing His identity—"I am the light of the world"—Jesus emphasized the importance of our proximity: "Anyone who follows me." The word Jesus used for *follow* means more than heeding navigational directions. Jesus was calling disciples who would pattern their lives after His and stay in close connection. He painted a picture of a shared journey.

It's a word that causes me to pause when I'm tempted to press through the day in my own strength or tackle problems with my solutions. Instead of plotting my direction, I'm reminded to prioritize connection: "How can I stick close to the Light of the World today?"

Sometimes sticking close looks like singing praise songs while driving across town or praying as I do the dishes. Other times it looks like opening my

Bible instead of opening my favorite app or rehearsing God's promises instead of ruminating on my worries.

There are countless ways to share the journey with Jesus, but they all involve heeding His directives and remaining alert to His presence. Because if we want a Savior to guide our steps, we must stay close enough to follow His.

JOURNAL PROMPT

What's one way you can stick close to the Light of the World today?

37

The Quickest Way to Overcome the Darkness

LAURA LACEY JOHNSON

The Messiah would suffer, and ...
as the first to rise from the dead, he would
proclaim light to our people and to the Gentiles.
ACTS 26:23

During my first year of college, I learned that our university president had a fun tradition. He wanted to show students he cared for them, so he and his family hosted informal popcorn parties on the back porch of their home.

Munching on popcorn with the president and my friends always infused joy into my heart. Those evenings overflowed with laughter, games, and light-hearted antics. But my favorite part was anticipating the invitation, looking for the signal.

Whenever the president flipped on a bright blue light on the balcony of his three-story campus home, it was a moment of great anticipation and delight. Everyone knew they had an invitation to come. Students tried to predict when the blue light would glow, and watching for this light became a thrilling game. As one upperclassman taught me during my first week on campus, "Watch for the light because that's your invite!"

We all love to get invitations. God created us with a desire for belonging and connection tucked deep inside of us. Today's passage reveals a golden invitation for each of us to come to the light of Christ.

Acts 26:23 is more than a verse; it's an invitation from the heart of God to step into the light of His love. This verse beckons us to come to the light, let it flood every corner of our lives, and transform us from the inside out. In this verse, the apostle Paul described Jesus Christ as "the first to rise from the dead" and as one who "would proclaim light to our people and to the Gentiles." These two descriptions contain powerful implications for us all.

When Paul spoke of Jesus as "the first to rise from the dead," he wasn't merely recounting a fact—he was unveiling the pathway to eternal life with Christ—a doorway swung wide open for you and me. Jesus was the first to rise from the dead because, unlike previous resurrections such as Lazarus and those raised by Elijah and Elisha, the miraculous display of God's power in Christ provided a permanent solution for sin and death. Lazarus and the others eventually had to die again. But Jesus' resurrection proved His power to conquer death and grant eternal life without end (Romans 6:8–9).

Paul also declared that the light isn't just for a select few or for those who have it all together. Instead, this light is for everyone—the Jew and the Gentile, the seeker and the skeptic, the orphaned and the hopeless. Through Jesus, we have an invitation to experience abundant life, freedom from darkness and shame, and unshakable hope, which can be found only in Him. Paul's message is clear: Because of Christ's death and resurrection, Jesus is a light for all, and He invites everyone to come to His light.

Sometimes we can get so distracted with our to-do lists that we need to be reminded of the extraordinary power of inviting people to experience Christ's light. All around us are people desperate for the light and love of Jesus that

> dispels darkness,
>
> breaks chains of bondage, and
>
> offers a fresh start.

My college president taught me the power of turning on a light and welcoming everyone. Who do you know who has experienced the darkness of discouragement? Who is desperate for words of life and light? Who needs Christ's love to rescue them from secrecy and shame?

The quickest way to extinguish the darkness is to flip on the light—the transformative power of Christ's light. By turning on the light for others, you'll often discover more of its radiance for yourself.

JOURNAL PROMPT

What is one way you can illuminate the light and love of Christ for someone in your life today?

_____

_____

_____

_____

_____

_____

38

We Have Seen His Glory

ALICIA BRUXVOORT

After six days Jesus took Peter, James, and his brother John and led them up on a high mountain by themselves. He was transfigured in front of them, and his face shone like the sun; his clothes became as white as the light.

MATTHEW 17:1–2

"If I had known who he was, I would've listened," one of my favorite students admitted when he stopped by my classroom to explain why he would be sitting in detention after school instead of attending my book club. His story spilled out between grumbles and sighs. After getting stuck in traffic, he'd attempted to beat the tardy bell by sprinting to class. However, as he was racing through the crowded hallway, he heard a voice commanding, "Slow down!"

With a quick glance over his shoulder, he spotted a man wearing a sweatshirt adorned with the school logo. Assuming it was the gym teacher, he dismissed the directive to adjust his pace.

Turns out, the voice belonged to the principal.

Not surprisingly, my fast-footed favorite was promptly called to the office and issued a detention slip for ignoring the principal's instructions. When I asked what he'd learned from his encounter, my student gave me a contrite smile and said, "I need to pay attention when the principal speaks."

I wonder if that's what Jesus' friends were thinking when they got an unexpected glimpse of God's glory on a mountaintop one long-ago day. Matthew 17:1–2 chronicles the moment like this:

> After six days Jesus took Peter, James, and his brother John and led them up on a high mountain by themselves. He was transfigured in front of them, and his face shone like the sun; his clothes became as white as the light.

It's difficult to imagine what it looked like when the perfection of heaven was made visible on the dust of earth. But it's easy to imagine that after seeing the fullness of God's nature expressed in the frame of Jesus, Peter, James, and John suddenly understood how vital it was to pay attention to the man with whom they'd been sharing meals and miles, miracles and missions.

In that long-ago moment on the mountain, God's glory revealed Christ's identity and authority. And in our here-and-now moments of life, God's glory does the same.

It may not look like a dazzling light, but we can spot God's glory in the beauty of a sunrise or the tenacity of a sprouting seed, in the kindness of an act of mercy or the marvel of an answered prayer.

Of course, God doesn't display His glory merely to impress our eyes. He reveals His worth to enlist our ears. Perhaps that's why Christ's transfiguration was followed by a simple declaration: "This is my beloved Son, with whom I am well-pleased. Listen to him!" (Matthew 17:5). God's glory won't transform our story if we don't allow His words to instruct our steps. So next time we get a glimpse of God's heart, let's listen for His voice too.

Because—as my fast-footed student learned—when we know who He is, we're wise to heed what He says.

JOURNAL PROMPT

Where have you glimpsed God's glory lately? What's one way you can respond to what your eyes have seen?

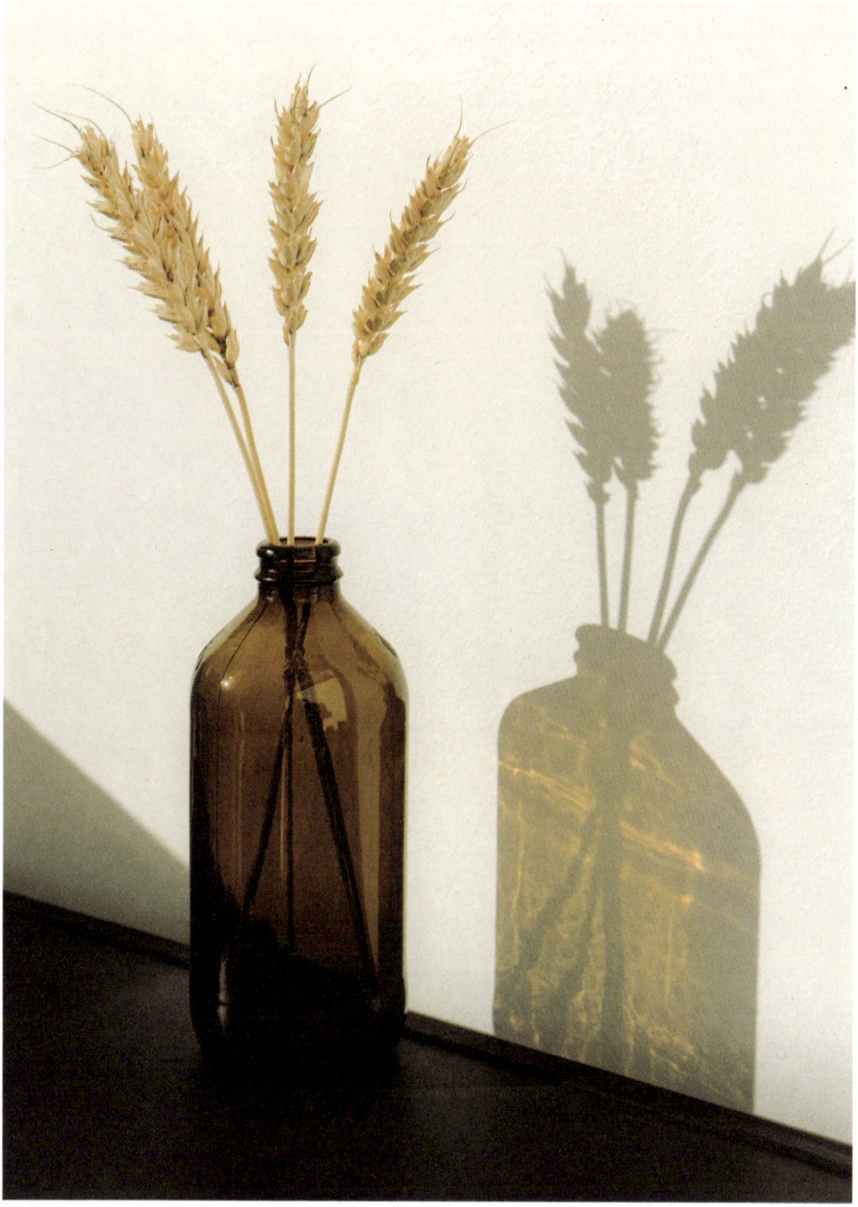

PART 8

Children of Light, Called to Shine

As followers of Jesus, we have a new identity: children of God. With God's Spirit living in us, we are called to shine God's light everywhere we go. We aren't walking in darkness, but the light. We are called to let our light shine so others will give glory to God and be drawn to the light for themselves.

39

Shine Pretty Shine

MEGHAN MELLINGER

No one lights a lamp and puts it under a basket, but rather on a lampstand, and it gives light for all who are in the house. In the same way, let your light shine before others, so that they may see your good works and give glory to your Father in heaven.

MATTHEW 5:15–16

"What's today's date?"

Out of the twenty kids sitting on the floor of a small schoolhouse in South Africa, one brave six-year-old girl wearing a pink sweatshirt raised her hand. My mission trip team and I watched as she approached the chalkboard, correctly arranged some cut-out numbers and words and turned to face her peers.

The entire room burst into jazz hands while shouting a phrase of applause that was new to me but known to them: "Shine pretty shine!"

It felt like I was watching a Broadway musical.

I'm not going to lie, life would be a lot more fun if I had a chorus of kids cheering me on every time I did something right, like actually driving the speed limit or eating a vegetable. But perhaps what I like most about this classroom's unique applause is the phrase "shine pretty shine."

It reminds me of the worthy work we have been called to in Matthew 5:15–16: "No one lights a lamp and puts it under a basket, but rather on a lampstand, and it gives light for all who are in the house. In the same way, let your light shine before others, so that they may see your good works and give glory to your Father in heaven."

As children of the Light of the World, we are called to shine Jesus' light in our world.

This assignment feels weighty, intimidating even. Such a significant responsibility for such a seemingly insignificant person. All eyes on you and me for the correct response.

I feel unqualified.

But there's beauty in this heavenly burden when we understand the context of these verses.

Lamps in those times were small. So to ensure maximum illumination, the lamp was placed on a stand to give "light for all who are in the house." Even though the light was small, when placed in the right position, it made the difference between a dark space and a house full of light.

While we may feel insignificant and unqualified, when we show up in the spaces and places we're divinely planted in, we can have a huge impact on all those in our "house," our sphere of influence. Even the smallest light can make a big impact.

It's not about living perfectly. We could read our "good works" as doing all the right things all the time. But in our humanness, we have the best opportunity to point to the divine. We can do this even in our anger and hurt, in our fear and frustration, in our sadness and desperation.

People are watching to see who we turn to for comfort, guidance, and hope. It is not about always doing good but about calling upon the One who is good. Our calling is not to be perfect but to point to the perfect One. We're not here to bring praise to ourselves through our actions but to actively bring praise to Jesus. To point to, direct attention toward, applaud, and glorify Him.

Or as the second definition in Merriam-Webster's online dictionary entry for *glorify* says: "to light up brilliantly."

To shine pretty shine.

What a humbling calling it is to brilliantly light up Jesus in all areas of our lives for all those in our lives.

JOURNAL PROMPT

Who is a part of your "house," your sphere of influence and impact? In what ways can you position yourself to shine Jesus' light to make the most impact for them?

40

The Antidote to Identity Theft

MEREDITH HOUSTON CARR

For you were once darkness, but now you are light in the Lord.
Walk as children of light.
EPHESIANS 5:8

My youngest child has a profoundly tender and sensitive heart. She longs to do what's right, but like any headstrong seven-year-old (or middle-aged mama), sometimes her sinful nature takes over.

After a recent sibling spat, I found her crying in her room. Though the quarrel had been resolved and forgiven, my little girl still wailed into her pillow. When I asked her what was wrong, she sobbed, "I did a bad thing, Mama, which means *I am bad*!"

At that moment, my own tender heart broke for hers, for how often have I done the same soul math of equating my mistakes with my identity?

Maybe you have too. Perhaps it's a past mistake that plays endlessly in your mind—or careless words spoken in a rash moment that still ring in your head. Maybe a moment of anger overtook your sanity, and the shame of remembering still turns your cheeks red.

It's no accident that we, like my daughter, tend to equate *who we are* with *what we've done,* because we have an Enemy who's hell-bent on hijacking our identities as children of God. His mission is quite literally "to steal and kill and destroy" (John 10:10).

One of our Enemy's favorite ways to fulfill his sinister mission is by attacking the core of *who* we are. When guilt and shame from past mistakes and imperfections loom, we shrink back into the dark. Instead of walking boldly in faith, we hide away.

Our Enemy may be an identity thief, but we aren't powerless against him! The simple, daily act of recalling and remembering our one true identity acts as an antidote to the Enemy's schemes. Today's key verse acts as an "identification card" of sorts, reminding us of who we are and what we're called to do on this earth:

> For you were once darkness, but now you are light in the Lord. Walk as children of light. (Ephesians 5:8)

With confident clarity, Paul's words remind us that we are no longer the darkness we once walked in. In Christ, we not only have light—we *are* light! So while you may have mishaps and mistakes in your past and present, you are not defined by them.

The salvation and redemption Jesus accomplished for us on the cross don't rise and fall on our perfection or behavior. We'll still battle our sinful nature this side of heaven, but our new identity as children of His light empowers us to fight back.

Dear one, your humanity doesn't have to keep you from shining His light, for even when you mess up, it's an opportunity to display God's mercy, grace, and forgiveness to a world in desperate need of those attributes. You don't have to be perfect to let your light shine, because the perfection of *the* Light never falters, even when we do. So remember *who* and *whose* you are—and walk boldly as a child of light!

JOURNAL PROMPT

Write Ephesians 5:8 on a small note card, and place it somewhere you'll see it each morning (like your bathroom mirror or your car's dashboard). Then journal a prayer you can pray whenever the Enemy's lies tempt you to hide your light instead of shining brightly for Jesus.

_____

_____

_____

_____

_____

41

Prepared for the Storm

ASHLEY MORGAN JACKSON

Jesus answered, "The light will be with you only a little longer. Walk while you have the light so that darkness doesn't overtake you. The one who walks in darkness doesn't know where he's going. While you have the light, believe in the light so that you may become children of light."

JOHN 12:35–36

Growing up, I always loved thunderstorms. I loved the excitement of not knowing what would happen, watching for lightning and then counting the seconds before the clap of the thunder. It was all very thrilling, especially because it was rare in the California desert where I was raised.

But occasionally there was a storm that wasn't so cozy, and I stopped feeling safe. These were the times when the power would go out and we no longer had access to our source of light. We stood frozen, as silence and darkness fell on us. We could not see one single thing.

My mom always seemed prepared in these moments. She would tell us to stay where we were and wait for her. She knew where the matches were and would find and light every candle in the house until we could see again.

Sometimes life can feel dark and scary like this, can't it? But Jesus isn't surprised. In fact, He is the solution.

In John 12:35–36 Jesus said, "The light will be with you only a little longer. Walk while you have the light so that darkness doesn't overtake you. The one who walks in darkness doesn't know where he's going. While you have the light, believe in the light so that you may become children of light."

His Word tells us that we do not have to be like the one overtaken by darkness, frozen in fear or screaming in confusion. No, Jesus calls us to be prepared with His light of truth by being in His Word, daring to believe it, and living it out. In this way, we make ourselves ready for times of darkness so we can see where we must go and so we can hold out that light for others.

My mom didn't know when our electricity would be knocked out, but she was prepared for it. As she lived day to day in the light, she placed candles around the house and tucked matches where she could find them. She was prepared for the times when we could not find our way.

Oh, friend, we can be ready in the same way. Storms will come, and the darkness of this world will surround us, but we have access to the light. We can take the necessary steps to have what we need by knowing God's truth and holding it up as our guide when things become unclear.

As we walk in the light with Jesus, we become like Him, and even when darkness falls, we will not be overcome by it.

JOURNAL PROMPT

Take a few moments to think of how God may ask you to hold out your light to a world lost in the dark. (It could be as simple as serving at church, being kind to the cashier, or befriending a fellow parent at school.) Jot down a simple prayer for those people, and ask the Lord to help you walk as His child of the light.

42

The Light of Life Lives in You

JUNE CHAPMAN

In him was life, and that life was the light of men. That light shines in the darkness, and yet the darkness did not overcome it.

JOHN 1:4–5

Three years ago, I joined a new Bible study group. I cried on my way there, feeling alone and filled with grief born from years of unexpected trials. My heart was skeptical that my situation would change, and there seemed to be no light at the end of my tunnel.

That was the day I met Katherine. While at the potluck salad bar, Katherine asked me one of life's simplest and most challenging questions if we answer honestly: "How are you?"

I was, perhaps, overly honest. This kind stranger listened patiently and then replied gently, "I'd love to hear more." I laid out the darkness in my life, and she didn't look away. Instead, our friendship blossomed. Katherine listened long and loved well. This believing sister became a beacon of hope, not just because of who she is but because of who lives inside her. In her was the Light.

In God's first act of creation, He said, "Let there be light" (Genesis 1:3). God's light filled the darkness of the world. But He didn't stop there. As we read in the book of John, Jesus came to shine God's light into the darkness of hearts. The disciple wrote, "In him was life, and that life was the light of men. That light shines in the darkness, and yet the darkness did not overcome it" (John 1:4–5).

Christ's eternal light is at the end of all our darkest tunnels. And it's also inside *us*. Just like He lives in Katherine, He lives in you. In those steepest valleys of sorrow and those deepest canyons of disappointment, His light illuminates the trenches of our hearts because He is our life.

When we follow His light, He will give us the strength to believe His promise: The darkness will never overcome Him. We can look for the glimmers of hope in the dark places and remember the King is coming back. And our promise of hope isn't just for the future. Jesus came in the flesh and died on the cross to give us life anew even *before* that second coming. He came to the world so that we might have full and abundant life amid the Enemy's wicked scheming (John 10:10).

We can live in this promise because the Light who laid down His life for us lives inside us and in the guiding Word He's given us.

Jesus offers us fullness of joy in His presence. Knowing and experiencing Him is our comfort and our hope. He sanctifies, encourages, and counsels. He is a light the Enemy cannot extinguish.

In the Lord's precious gift of Katherine's friendship, He reminded me that I was not alone. He wanted to meet me right where I was—in His Word and through the sweet believers around me. No matter how dark things seemed, the darkness could not win.

In heaven, our hearts won't suffer dark nights. Caverns of grief will be transformed into fields of glory. Until then, we have the Light of life and glimmers of His goodness. That Light has a name: Jesus. And the Light lives in us.

JOURNAL PROMPT

Reflect on areas of sin or circumstances in your life that feel exceedingly dark. How might you lean into Christ's presence and guidance in His Word to renew hope and run your race with perseverance? Ask the Lord to let you notice the glimmers of His goodness and to remind you that His light will not be overcome.

43

Living Lanterns

BRENDA BRADFORD OTTINGER

What I tell you in the dark, speak in the light. What you hear in a whisper, proclaim on the housetops.

MATTHEW 10:27

Perhaps you, too, have spent years of your life unaware of the purpose breathed into you by God. Does the woman who met your eyes in the mirror this morning know she has a beautiful purpose in this world?

Reflecting further across history, let's peek into a scene where Jesus had something to say about purpose. Jesus instructed, "What I tell you in the dark, speak in the light. What you hear in a whisper, proclaim on the housetops" (Matthew 10:27).

You see, in the quiet of their moments alone, Jesus imparted divine insight to His disciples. Now Jesus told them it was time to take those hidden whispers from Him and openly proclaim them from the housetops.

Jesus' use of the word *housetops* refers to the fact that most rooftops at the time were flat, providing perfect platforms for voices to carry through the streets. With this mandate, Jesus breathed purpose into His followers, sending them forth as living lanterns to shine His heart from the risers of their lives.

Again, after His resurrection and before His ascension to heaven, Jesus repeated this call, saying, "Make disciples of all nations . . . teaching them to observe everything I have commanded you" (Matthew 28:19–20).

Oh, how these words from the Savior echo through the centuries and meet us in this modern moment! Still today, Jesus imparts divine insight to His followers as He beckons us to sit at His hem, gathering His whispers to proclaim throughout the world. What beautiful purpose the Lord has spoken into our lives: this timeless mandate from antiquity, still calling our generation to carry the whispers of the Savior to the next.

In the quiet of your time with the Lord, may you sense His invitation into an adventure of purpose with Him. That passion you cradle for a cause, that tug in your spirit to serve, those gifts dancing inside you that uniquely equip you to proclaim Jesus in the world—oh, that you'd hear His whispers of purpose in your soul to shine His heart from the platforms of your life.

Take heart. You don't need to be in the spotlight to shine His light, and your purpose isn't dependent on the size of your platform. Even those messages proclaimed from ancient rooftops allowed simply for those in their midst to hear.

Friend, those in your midst are your mission. Your life holds profound purpose, for right where you are, you're a living lantern, equipped by God to reflect Jesus in the world He spent His life to save.

JOURNAL PROMPT

In your quiet time with God, listen for His whispers of purpose. Where can you sense Him stirring your spirit to share His heart with the world?

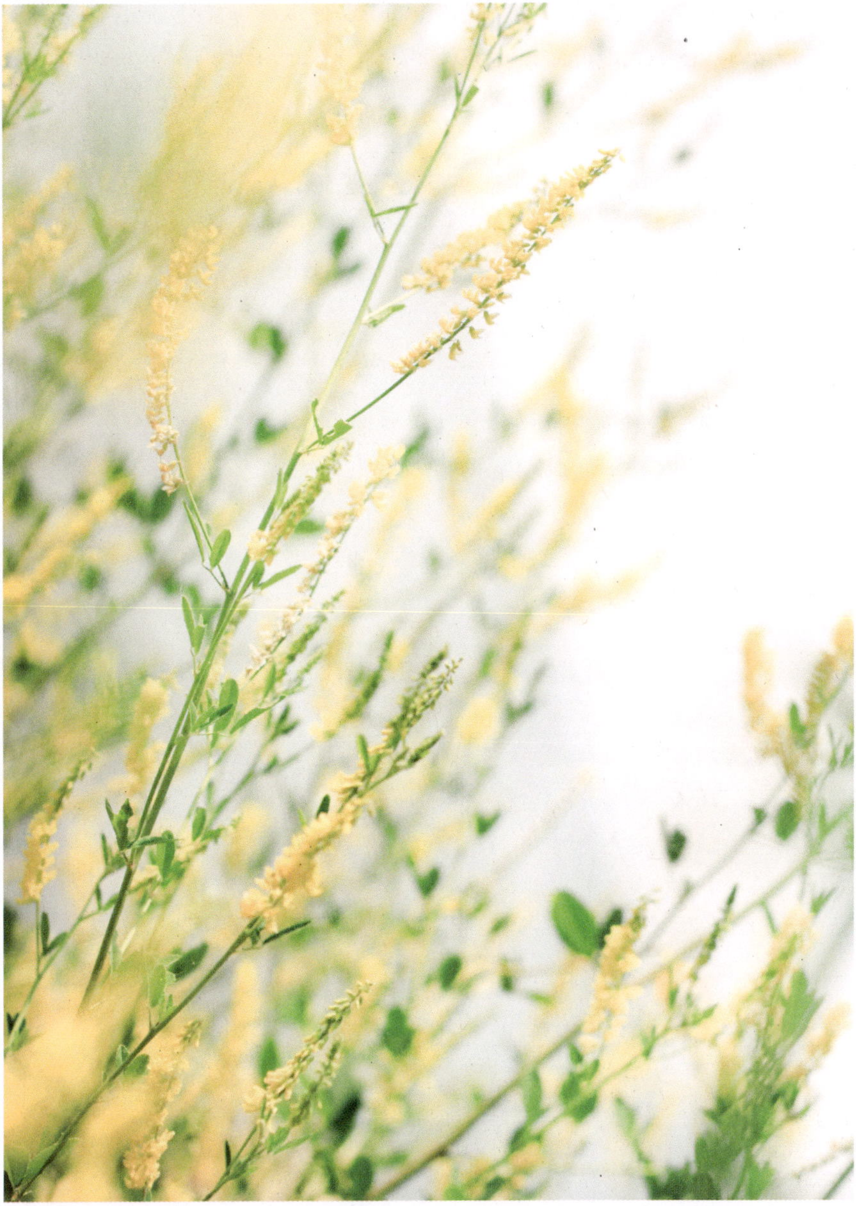

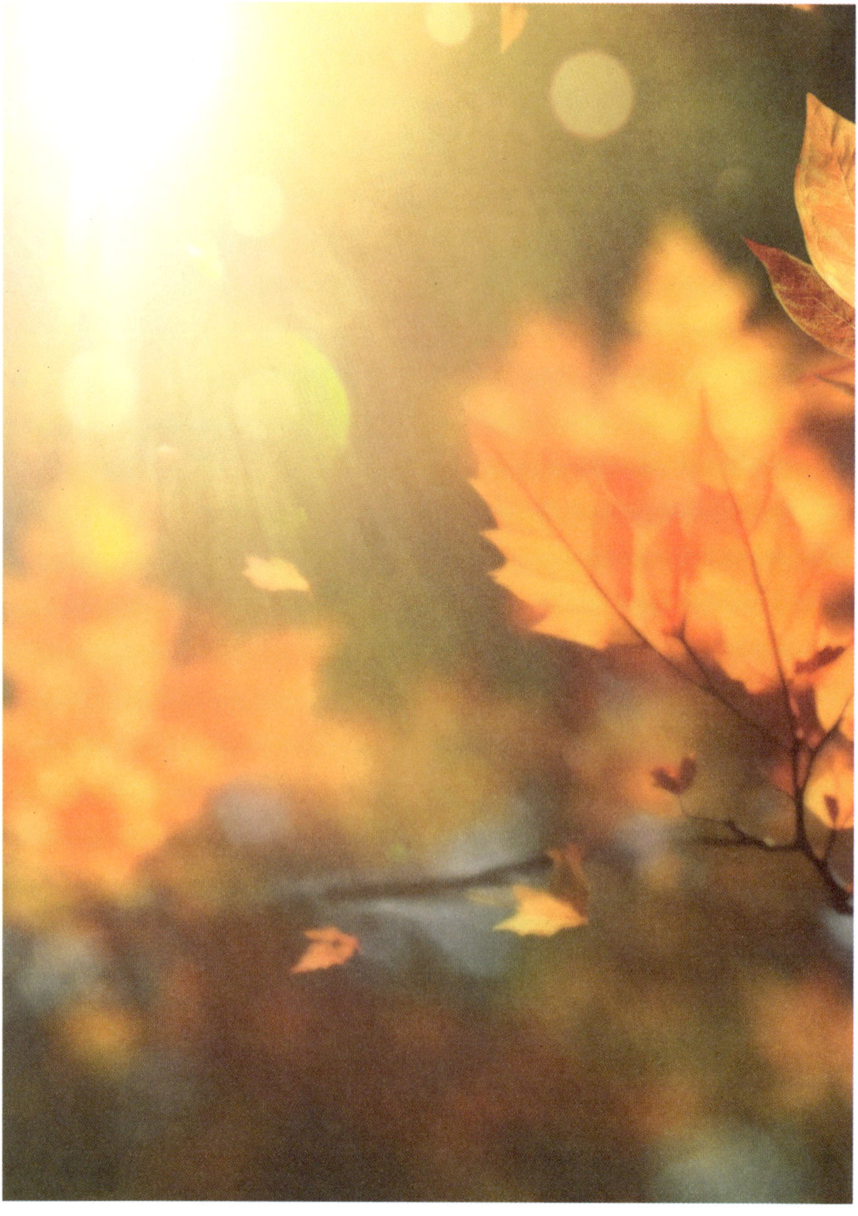

PART 9

Darkness Is Defeated

Two thousand years ago, Jesus came to earth and defeated death. Here's the good news: He's coming back. We are called to wait in anticipation, to be ready, to be watching for that day. On that day, God Himself will be our light. Everything will be clear. Darkness will be defeated—forever. Amen.

44
A New Day Is Dawning

SARAH FREYMUTH

*Let's strive to know the LORD. His appearance is
as sure as the dawn. He will come to us like the rain,
like the spring showers that water the land.*

HOSEA 6:3

Can you hear it? The hum of Him who is coming to make all things right?

Can you see it? The light piercing all darkness to shine righteousness like a thousand revolving suns?

Feel the pull of your heart longing for more. Longing to be made whole, restored.

The longing for light comes in the night, when fears amplify and feelings of loneliness seem overwhelming. But fear not, for dawn appears, cresting above the hill and illuminating the shadow-spotted world with pure, unfurling light.

We are a parched people, gulping down cheap distractions to satisfy a thirst for what we cannot find in this world. Perhaps we've lived too long in the underground, burrowing into our own desires and walking our own way. It's left us looking through a distorted image of love, self-worth, and security, and we wonder whether we can recover our losses.

Take heart, dear one. A way has been made through the wilderness, arising within our burning hearts: God's great light, given in abundance through the life, death, and resurrection of Jesus Christ.

It is never too late to turn to God's grace and mercy. His arms are wide open, waiting, wanting you to come to Him with a heart ready to receive all He offers.

> Let's strive to know the Lord.
> His appearance is as sure as the dawn.
> He will come to us like the rain,
> like the spring showers that water the land. (Hosea 6:3)

The Lord is coming, sure as the sun appears each morning. One day He will make all things new (Revelation 21:5), and "every knee will bow" and "every tongue will confess that Jesus Christ is Lord" (Philippians 2:10–11). We are waiting for the dawn of this new day. Our hearts cry out for it. We were made for eternity and to live in the light of God.

> The Lord is my light and my salvation—
> whom should I fear?
> The Lord is the stronghold of my life—
> whom should I dread? (Psalm 27:1)

The Lord is our light. There will be no need for sunlight or artificial light because God Himself will illuminate our days (Revelation 21:23). His peace will surround us, His love will embrace us, and we will be face-to-face with our Lord. What a glorious day that will be!

You are not too far gone to get in step with God. He is here, waiting to satisfy your parched heart and shower you with His refreshing love.

Prepare your heart for the coming King. Live in the light of His love; walk in goodness and mercy. Align your heart and mind to His kingdom, and let His light shine in your life. A new day is dawning.

JOURNAL PROMPT

Where do you need the dawn of God's grace in your life? How might you invite Him to let His light shine through you?

45

The Light of Christ Will Lead Us Home

RACHEL MARIE KANG

> *As [Saul] traveled and was nearing Damascus, a light from heaven suddenly flashed around him. Falling to the ground, he heard a voice saying to him, "Saul, Saul, why are you persecuting me?" "Who are you, Lord?" Saul said. "I am Jesus, the one you are persecuting," he replied.*
>
> ACTS 9:3–5

Not too long ago, I met up with a friend for coffee at a café.

We smiled and hugged, laughed, and shed a tear or two. And we talked and talked, unearthing the depths of our hearts. In time, my friend shared something weighing heavy in her life. A story of sorrow, secrets, and sin—the kind that festers and flourishes deep down in the dark.

We took turns talking. *She would confess. I would comfort her. She would confess. I would comfort her.* Then, when it was all said and done, we somehow managed to settle together on the same truth—how liberating it feels to step into the light.

Truth is, though I am a child of the light, I am no stranger to the darkness. I know what it's like, in the secret corridors of my heart, to have cursed my sister and coveted the life of my neighbor. In the dark places of my mind where no human hand can reach, I've hated and held grudges. I've harbored worry and fear, all while puffing myself up with pride.

But like a candle shining brightly in the darkness, the Lord can cut through every layer of sin and shadow, drawing us back to the kingdom of light. It is like Saul's encounter with the Lord on the road to Damascus. There he was—lost to life and lost to Christ until, suddenly, a bright light flashed and surrounded him. Startled, he fell to the ground and heard a voice say, "Saul, Saul, why are you persecuting me?" (Acts 9:4).

There, in his darkness, Saul was found . . . and found out. A bright light shone all around him, captivating him, catching his attention, and drawing him to hear and heed the Lord. Still, the light of Christ is not simply a glory show. More than *captivatingly* bright, the light of Christ is an *illuminating* light. For it is not enough for Jesus to capture our attention. He wants to lead us to confession and affection. He wants to lead us home, turning our hearts to Him.

On the road to Damascus, the Lord shone a light so bright that Saul couldn't focus on anything else other than what the Lord laid a finger upon. "I am Jesus, the one you are persecuting," said the Lord (Acts 9:5). From persecuting Jesus to preaching Him, Saul wasn't merely captivated by the light of Christ; he was changed and called by it.

The light of Christ doesn't just lay us down; it leads us home. It is a bright light that burns away all sin and shame, but never to harm or humiliate. The light of Christ burns bright to bring us back to Himself.

Right back to His loving arms . . . where we've always belonged.

JOURNAL PROMPT

In this season of life, what kind of encounter do you need with God? Do you need the light of the Lord to captivate your attention or to illuminate your sins? In what state would He find your heart? What habits or actions would He call to your attention?

46

Living in Anticipation

CARRIE ZEILSTRA

Besides this, since you know the time, it is already the hour for you to wake up from sleep, because now our salvation is nearer than when we first believed. The night is nearly over, and the day is near; so let us discard the deeds of darkness and put on the armor of light.

ROMANS 13:11–12

Squeak, squeak, sque-e-e-a-k.

I pressed the green dry-erase marker to my bathroom mirror. A smile spread across my sleepy face as I stepped back to see my handiwork.

Gone was the number 24 I had written yesterday. Now the number 23 stared back at me.

Twenty-three more days!

This had been part of my morning routine for several months. When I started my countdown, the green number had three digits. Now I was just over three weeks away from the highly anticipated event.

I often have a countdown going—for vacations, conferences, or big life events. When we were engaged, my husband even made me a paper chain to count down the days until our wedding.

Someone once challenged this habit, asking if my need to look ahead meant that I was not content to live in the present.

After some prayer and reflection, God showed me the benefits of my countdowns.

Looking ahead doesn't mean I am wishing away the present. Instead, looking ahead gives me *hope* in hard moments, helps me stay *focused* on my goals, and reminds me of my *purpose* while I wait.

However, through that reflection, God pointed me toward the truth that I have more to look forward to than just vacations, conferences, and fun events. I have eternity with Him, which is drawing nearer each day.

> Besides this, since you know the time, it is already the hour for you to wake up from sleep, because now our salvation is nearer than when we first believed. The night is nearly over, and the day is near; so let us discard the deeds of darkness and put on the armor of light. (Romans 13:11–12)

Paul reminded the early church that though they had received salvation when they believed in Christ, their deliverance from the darkness of this world was still on the horizon.

We are in that same place today. Even after we believe in Jesus, we still live in a broken world, surrounded by darkness. But a day is coming when we will be *with* the Lord.

We can't count down to this glorious day, since we don't know the exact day or time (Matthew 24:36). However, we *can* lift our eyes beyond the lesser things of this earth and look forward to what is coming.

This attitude of expectation should make us live differently. Looking toward our salvation should fill us with hope, focus, and purpose. There is purpose in today, even as we wait for the day of our salvation. We turn our backs to the darkness and "put on the armor of light" (Romans 13:12).

Later in Romans 13, Paul repeated this idea when he said, "*Put on* the Lord Jesus Christ" (v. 14, italics added).

Imagine stepping into the thoughts and actions of Christ. Pulling our arms through the sleeves of Christlikeness, like a uniform that shows we are His. Setting His eternal perspective on our heads. Marching into the battles of the day with the light of our Savior leading the charge.

Each day, we choose light over darkness. And we "put on the armor of light," stepping into our daily routine with joyful expectation. One day closer to the eternal light of the glory of our Lord.

One hour closer.

One breath closer.

JOURNAL PROMPT

What would it look like for you to live with anticipation of your salvation? By choosing to "put on" Jesus, what darkness do you need to let go of?

47

Finding Purpose in the Pause

ASHLEY MORGAN JACKSON

At that time the kingdom of heaven will be like ten virgins who took their lamps and went out to meet the groom. Five of them were foolish and five were wise.

MATTHEW 25:1–2

"Is it time yet, Lord?" I asked for what felt like the hundredth time in the past few years. I knew God was good, I knew He loved me, I knew I could trust Him, but I didn't understand why He was making me wait.

I thought I had heard Him correctly about what He wanted for my life, the direction He wanted me to go, yet it seemed nothing was changing; there was no movement, just . . . waiting.

Maybe you know the pain of waiting as well. Waiting for a relationship. Waiting for a job. Waiting for a baby. Waiting for things in your life to make sense again. It is hard to keep holding on to hope when the wait is long.

But, friend, while we may not know when God will move, be ready, keep looking, because He is on His way.

Matthew 25:1–2 says, "At that time the kingdom of heaven will be like ten virgins who took their lamps and went out to meet the groom. Five of them were foolish and five were wise." These ten bridesmaids were waiting with their lamps for the groom to arrive. Some were foolish, not having enough oil to wait longer, while others were wise and prepared themselves for however long it would take.

We are meant to be like these wise women who represent the bride of Christ waiting for Jesus' return, holding out the light of hope, ready with all we need to wait. We prepare our lights to last, to show us the way, and to give us hope in the wait. We may not know when the Lord will come through, but we can be prepared to wait well.

Sometimes waiting well looks like choosing trust again and again, cultivating our faith in the face of our pain, or declaring God's goodness despite our circumstances. With each choice, we are preparing ourselves by being reminded of who we are waiting on and why He is so worthy.

Oh, friend, know today that God is not indifferent to the pain of your wait. He sees, He cares, and He is with you. Your wait is not a punishment but an opportunity for preparation.

JOURNAL PROMPT

Take a few minutes to journal about something you have been waiting on and anything of significance you have learned about yourself, the Lord, or others while you have been in this wait.

_____

_____

_____

_____

_____

_____

_____

_____

_____

_____

48
Worshiping the Most High King over Every Lesser Thing

JUNE CHAPMAN

For as the lightning flashes from horizon to horizon and lights up the sky, so the Son of Man will be in his day.

LUKE 17:24

I am deeply grieved to the point of death," I wrote in my prayer journal, echoing Christ's words in the garden of Gethsemane (Matthew 26:38). But I was processing my own pain—sorrow over a situation that had ended disastrously.

As I journaled and prayed, the Lord began illuminating a hard truth: I had created an idol. I had set something in a high place where it didn't belong. It crashed to the ground, and the shattered pieces flew like poison arrows through my heart. I had directed my time, affection, and attention—all my worship—toward my idol, as though it would bring me fullness of joy.

As believers, we will discover that idols never satisfy. In this realization, we can long for the ultimate fulfillment of Christ's return. Even now, we try to restore joy that sin has marred and we desire broken things to be healed.

In Luke 17, Jesus addressed this longing. He delivered a warning against worshiping false gods in the anticipation of His return: "They will say to you, 'See there!' or 'See here!' Don't follow or run after them" (v. 23).

We'll know it's really Him because He told us: "For as the lightning flashes from horizon to horizon and lights up the sky, so the Son of Man will be in his day" (v. 24).

We might not be tempted to worship false prophets, but what about the ideals of comfort, financial security, control, or popularity? Or perhaps people, their opinions, or their approval? It's tempting to elevate things we desire to places of piety. These things may offer promises of satisfaction or joy; they may be enticing, beckoning us to seek them first. The Enemy longs to see us worship things that are not God.

Jesus told us not to put lesser things in His place while we wait for Him. He said "follow me," knowing that lesser gods would always let us down (Luke 9:23).

When our true King comes, we will know. From east to west, the sky will be filled with His glory. His grandeur is unmatched, and His coming will be unrivaled. We won't be tempted to wonder if any lesser thing could have stood in His place.

His is the majestic light that is unchanging, unfailing, and undivided. When Jesus is our priority, His light reveals the false promises of idols. Just as He will one day illuminate the horizon as if by lightning, He is the source of truth in our lives now.

My idol promised to light up my life, but it only stole my attention. When I redirected my worship to Jesus, I saw my situation for what it was: a lesser thing in light of my higher King. His mercy flowed into my garden of grief, and He illuminated my darkened hope. I realized that Jesus was the only worthy light of my heart. No lesser thing gave its life for me.

We may glimpse now only the glow of the glory of God that will one day surpass even the sun's brightness. But the Light of the World is coming. Jesus will light up the sky.

JOURNAL PROMPT

Are you occasionally tempted to seek fulfillment in something or someone other than Jesus? Reflect on God's glory and goodness, and consider ways you might find the light of your life in Him. Remember that when He returns, the lesser things will pale in comparison to the unimaginable joy He has promised.

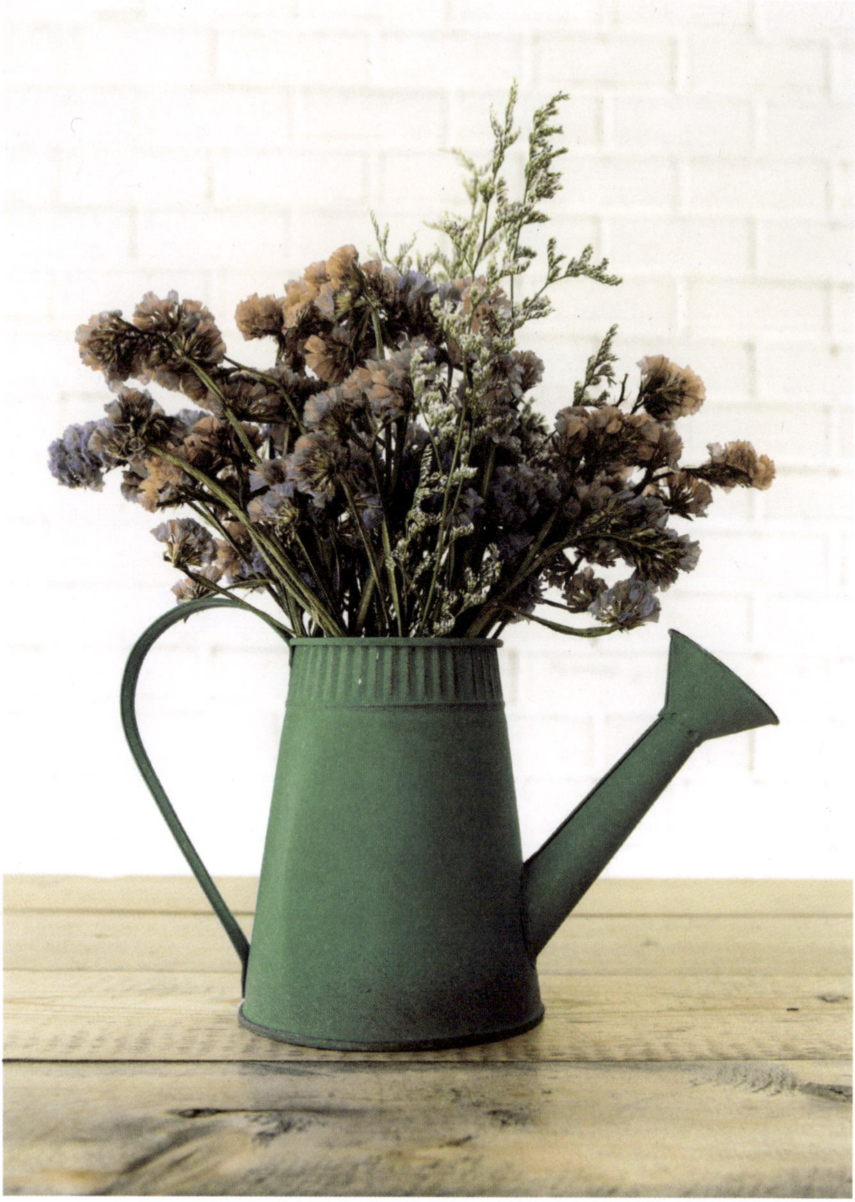

49

Our New "Irreversible"

HADASSAH TREU

Night will be no more; people will not need the light of a lamp or the light of the sun, because the Lord God will give them light, and they will reign forever and ever.

REVELATION 22:5

Friend, what is your "irreversible"? Irreversible losses and unresolved situations on this earth, the ones beyond repair, often have the power to plunge us into the darkness of hopelessness. They reach deep down in our souls to the springs of life and threaten to freeze them.

It is wonderful when we experience the Lord's deliverance and salvation right here, right now. But what is our hope when this is not the case? How can we still await the future with joyful expectation when the unthinkable happens and our worst-case scenarios materialize?

I look at the photos of us holding hands and smiling, and the pain of the devastating loss cuts like a knife through my stomach. My happy and cherished life with my closest person is gone forever. It seems impossible to imagine a happy life again; it is difficult to hope that good days will come.

Will I find joy again after this heavy sorrow? Will I again have a life I cherish, overflowing with blessings?

I want to know if there will be "again" in my life.

Perhaps you ask these questions, too, when you face life-altering, irreversible losses like permanent damage to your health, a shattered dream, or losing a loved one.

In my wrestling with the Lord, He faithfully guided me to the truth in this verse: "Night will be no more; people will not need the light of a lamp or the light of the sun, because the Lord God will give them light, and they will reign forever and ever" (Revelation 22:5).

There will be an "again" in our lives because God will be our light again. There is one thing we can never lose, and this is the light of His presence.

Not only will we never lose it, but we will experience the presence of the Lord in a completely new, intense way. In our earthly lives, we perceive His light piercing the darkness of sin, pain, and suffering. But here God promises us something else: the absence of night!

There will be no darkness at all—physical, emotional, or spiritual. We will bathe completely in the bright light of the Lord God. His presence will saturate everything so there will be no need for any other source of light.

Can you imagine? God's light permeating every atom of your being, filling you with the ecstasy of inexplicable joy?

In our church, we often sing and talk about Jesus being enough and how we have everything in Him. When we face the agony of irreversible losses, we can often wonder if God's presence is enough to fill the emptiness inside. But

God promises a day when the unrestrained presence of the Lord will fill to the brim our empty spaces and satisfy our deepest longings.

One day everything will make sense. All pieces will come into place, making this new creation order irreversible. We will embrace our new irreversible, and we will reign (Revelation 5:9–10).

As sharers in God's glorious light, we will also share in His power, authority, and sovereignty as we could never imagine. But here and now we need to bridge the gap by faith, focusing on the glorious future and the all-present hope we have in Jesus.

JOURNAL PROMPT

How do you imagine your future? Can you trust the Lord with your irreversible losses? Ask the Lord to sanctify your imagination and to give you a vision of the glorious future that awaits you.

_____

_____

_____

_____

_____

_____

_____

_____

_____

50

From Solar-Powered to God-Powered

CARRIE ZEILSTRA

The city does not need the sun or the moon to shine on it, because the glory of God illuminates it, and its lamp is the Lamb.

REVELATION 21:23

"Get. Down. From. There," I grunted through clenched teeth, tugging the fabric with each word until finally it came down.

Wiping the sweat from my forehead, I stepped over the mound of dark-colored drapery now lying on the hardwood floor.

We had just received the keys to our new house. But before moving in a single piece of furniture, I was determined to uncover the large picture window that took up most of the wall.

"Who wants to keep light out?" I asked my husband when he questioned why I took down the expensive-looking drapes.

"Well, certainly not you!" he said, laughing.

We have now lived in our house for over a decade, and I love seeing sunlight pour in from every inch of that picture window.

I love light. I joke that I am solar-powered, but honestly, it's not too far from the truth. In fact, we all are solar-powered! Our earthly bodies depend on the sun, which provides food, boosts our mood, and gives us warmth. In biblical times, people relied even more on sunlight for daily routines.

The sun is evidence that our heavenly Father reveals glimpses of His character through His creation. The sun and moon are predictable and reliable. We know that God, who created the sun and moon, is infinitely trustworthy. God is greater than His creation and does not *need* what He created.

Revelation tells us that one day the glorious presence of God will be our source of light.

> The city does not need the sun or the moon to shine on it, because the glory of God illuminates it, and its lamp is the Lamb. (Revelation 21:23)

In the New Jerusalem, God's glory will illuminate every inch of our new home. Can you imagine?

This glorious light is the same light that lit the skies before God created the sun and moon (Genesis 1:2–17), that made Moses' face shine after he descended from the Lord's presence on Mount Sinai (Exodus 34:29). It is the same light that filled Solomon's temple (2 Chronicles 7:1) and illuminated the sky over the shepherds on the night of Christ's birth (Luke 2:9). The same light that changed Paul's heart and created in him a testimony that is still changing hearts today (Acts 9:1–6).

This wasn't just a powerful light source like the sun. This was the glory of the Lord momentarily breaking through the thin veil that separates us from our heavenly home.

We have not yet experienced the fullness of God's glory—the knock-you-off-your-feet, make-your-face-shine-for-days, life-changing glory of God. But we see in God's Word that it is *greater* than the greatest light source we have ever known.

It's hard for me to grasp the idea of the sun and moon being unnecessary. Yet a day is coming when we will dwell with the Light of the World, Jesus Christ, and the glory of our heavenly Father. On that day, we will no longer depend on the sun and moon. We will have everything we need in the glory of our heavenly Father and His Son, Jesus Christ!

JOURNAL PROMPT

The sun and moon teach us about God's trustworthiness. What other characteristics of God are reflected in His creation?

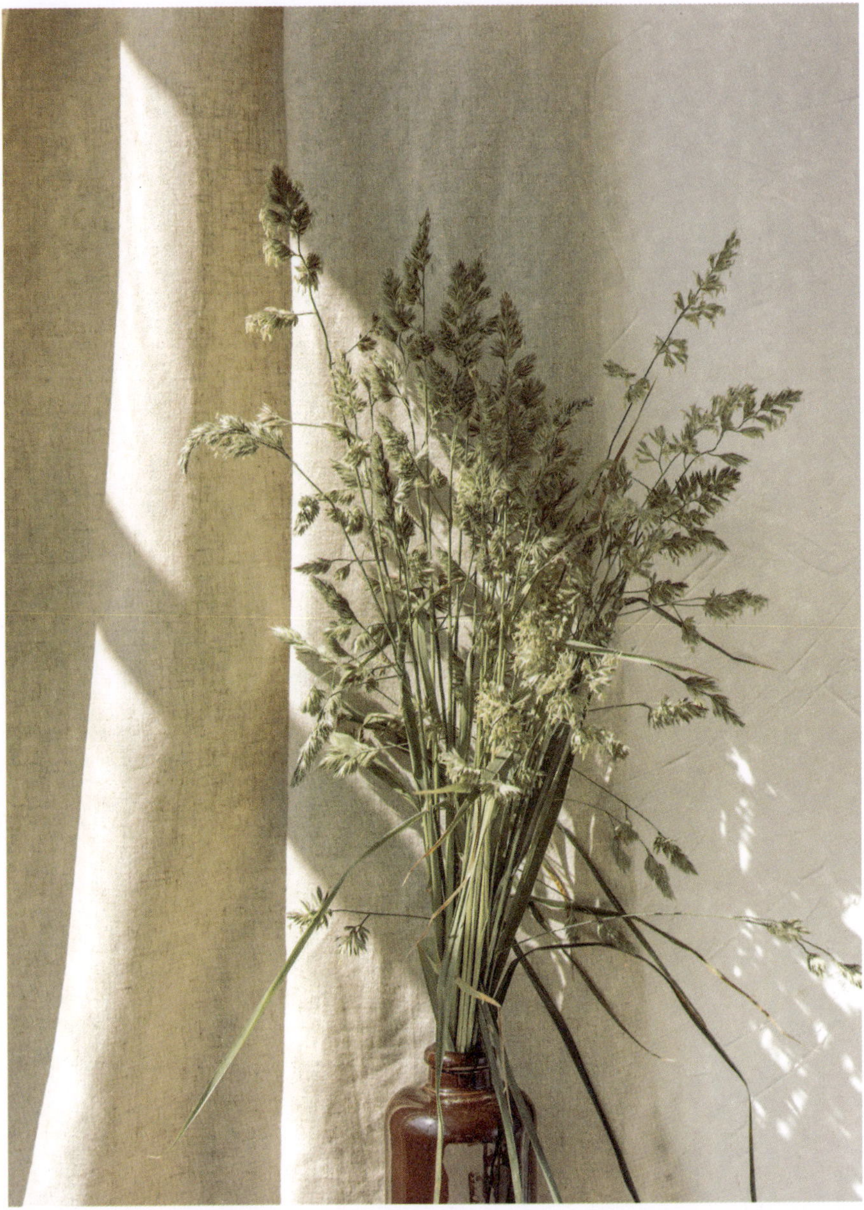

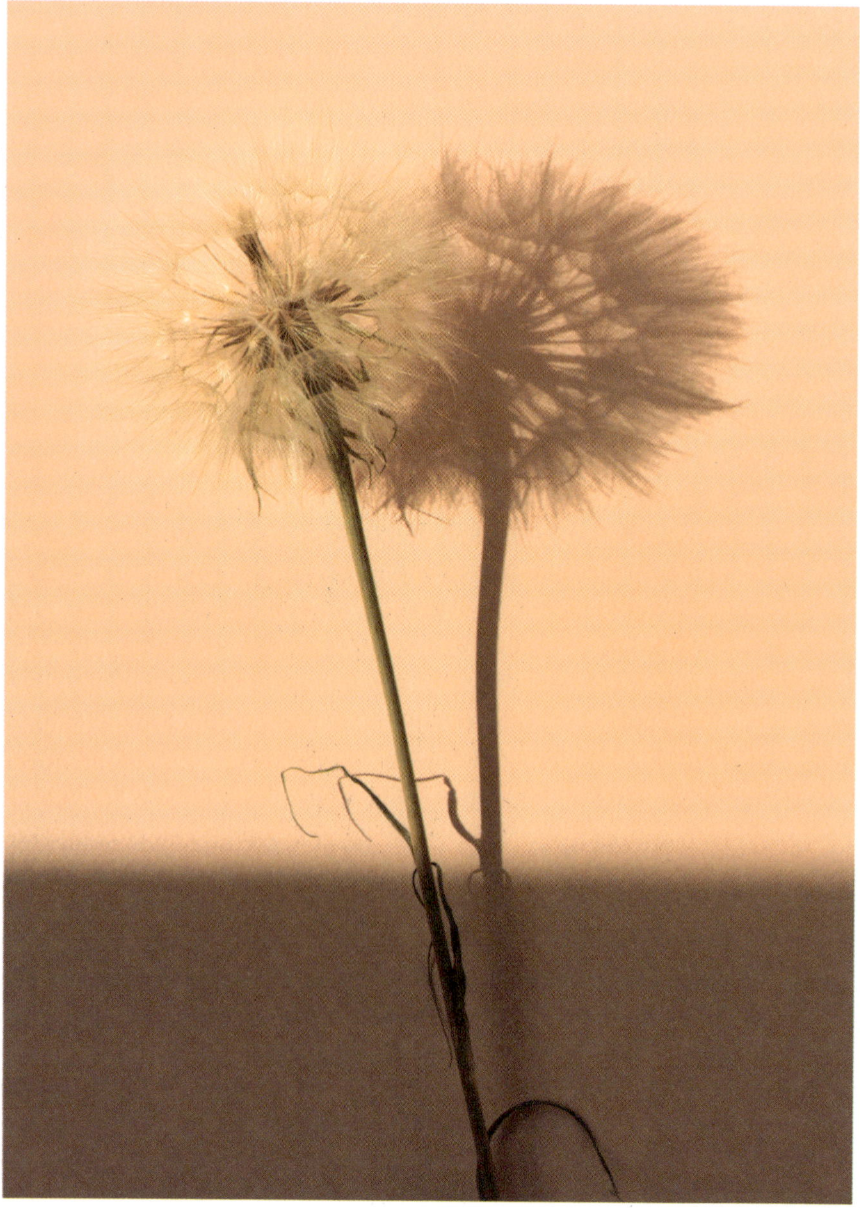

About the Writers

Wendy Blight is an author, Bible teacher, and attorney and serves as the biblical content specialist for Proverbs 31 Ministries. Her heart's desire is to connect women more deeply with God's Word: to learn it, pray it, and know with confidence that they can process any problem life presents through it. She loves spending time with her family, cooking, and watching college football. Wendy has authored five books. Her most recent book, *Rest for Your Soul: A Bible Study on Solitude, Silence & Prayer*, released in 2024. Wendy would love to connect with you at wendyblight.com.

Alicia Bruxvoort is a writer, speaker, and abundant-life seeker. She loves meeting Jesus on the pages of Scripture and helping others do the same. She serves on the devotion-writing team for Proverbs 31 Ministries and the teaching team at her local church. Alicia enjoys long walks in the woods, lively conversation around the dinner table, and sunny days at the beach. She's a storyteller at heart, but her favorite tale is the one she lives daily with her husband, Rob, and their growing family in Holland, Michigan. To connect with Alicia, visit her at aliciabruxvoort.net.

Meredith Houston Carr is a writer, speaker, and unrelenting dreamer. An attorney in her former life, she now enjoys the never-dull stay-at-home-mom life with her three energetic children. Meredith is passionately devoted to writing words that encourage and infuse women with hope—a hope that leads to the joy and strength needed to walk through life's hardships and into the abundant life promised by Jesus. After several adventure-filled years on the

West Coast, she and her husband now make their home in Athens, Georgia. To connect with Meredith, visit her at meredithhcarr.com.

June Chapman is the author of *Peace in the Waiting: When You Love People Who Don't Love God*. In her writing, June desires to point people to Christ's light in the darkness. She lives and works in the greater Washington, DC, area. June loves sharing the hope found in the gospel and has a heart for believers who are waiting to see their loved ones follow Jesus. She can also be found enjoying a good sandwich, spending time with her two cats, and exploring her city. Connect with June at junechapman.com.

Dr. Alicia Britt Chole is a leadership mentor, speaker, and award-winning writer whose works include *Anonymous: Jesus' Hidden Years . . . and Yours*, *40 Days of Decrease: A Different Kind of Hunger, A Different Kind of Fast*, and *The Night Is Normal: A Guide Through Spiritual Pain*. Dr. ABC directs Leadership Investment Intensives, Inc. (which provides custom, confidential soul care for leaders), and lives with her beloved family in the countryside off a dirt road. Her loves include honest questions, hot teas, thunderstorms, biographies, jalapeños, and travel. To connect with Alicia, visit aliciachole.com.

Asheritah Ciuciu is a national retreat speaker, YouTube Bible teacher, and bestselling author of ten books, including *Full: Food, Jesus, and the Battle for Satisfaction*, *Prayers of Rest: Daily Prompts to Slow Down and Hear God's Voice*, and *Unwrapping the Names of Jesus: An Advent Devotional*. Growing up as a Romanian missionary kid, Asheritah has always been passionate about helping people delight in Jesus through creative Bible habits. She and her high school sweetheart raise their three spunky kids in northeast Ohio. Connect with Asheritah and discover your devotional personality type at DelightinginJesus.com.

Claire Foxx serves as associate editor at Proverbs 31 Ministries and loves working with writers to teach God's Word and draw hearts to Jesus. She has also been a contributing writer for First 5 Bible study guides, including *Praying Through the Psalms: 30 Days to Uncomplicate How You Talk to God* and *Proverbs: Everyday Guidance for Making Everyday Decisions*. She holds a bachelor's degree in creative writing and a master's degree in English literature and lives in Charlotte, North Carolina, where local coffee shop staff know her on a first-name basis. She wouldn't have it any other way.

Sarah Freymuth is a writer and dreamer whose words breathe hope and wonder into the world. She enjoys being by Lake Michigan and her simple Midwest life with her husband and Beaglier pup, especially when they blend together on Washington Island. Sarah is the communications manager for Fellowship of Christian Athletes, writes for numerous publications, and is the editor of *Awake Our Hearts*, an online literary journal for the female voice exploring faith and life in full. Her book, *All the Hard Things: 50 Days Through the Valley*, releases in 2026. Connect with Sarah at sarahfreymuth.com.

Eric Gagnon is the author of *Good News: How the Four Gospels Point Us to One Person We Can Trust*. He has previously served as a pastor and now lives in the Charlotte, North Carolina, area, serving Proverbs 31 Ministries as a theological content specialist. He has a bachelor's degree in church ministry as well as a master's degree in theology from Gordon-Conwell Theological

Seminary. He is a husband to Sarah and a father of three. Find out more about Eric's ministry at adornthegospel.com.

Self-described as a divorce survivor and late-in-life thriver, Carole Holiday knows a thing or two about heartache. Carole authored her debut book, *I Don't Know Who I Am Anymore: Restoring Your Identity Shattered by Grief and Loss*, after an avalanche of loss threatened to steal her identity. Whether teaching cooking classes in a farmhouse cottage or sharing collaborative ventures with other writers, she tries to view life through the lens of other hurting women navigating life's griefs. A nana of nine, she delights in the treasures that can continually be uncovered for women over fifty. Visit caroleholiday.com to read her reflections or to leave your own.

Ashley Morgan Jackson is the bestselling author of *Tired of Trying: How to Hold On to God When You're Frustrated, Fed Up, and Feeling Forgotten*, a speaker, and a social media strategist with a heart for helping women break free from life's struggles to experience true spiritual growth. Through her writing and speaking, Ashley encourages women to get unstuck from unhealthy patterns and discover the freedom and joy found in Christ. Married for fifteen years, Ashley is also a devoted mom to two boys and loves bringing joy and laughter to everyday life. Connect with Ashley on Instagram @ashley.morgan.jackson for more faith-filled encouragement and inspiration.

Laura Lacey Johnson begins most mornings by sharing breakfast with students at College of the Ozarks, where her husband serves as president.

Laura speaks at women's retreats and has taught media writing, interpersonal communication, and fundamentals of speech communication at the collegiate level. Laura began her career as a radio personality and television news reporter. She is a featured author in *Clear Mind, Peaceful Heart: 50 Devotions for Sleeping Well in a World Full of Worry* and *Renew Your Mind: 40 Days to Quiet the Lies Inside Your Head*, published by Proverbs 31 Ministries. Visit her website at lauralaceyjohnson.com.

Rachel Marie Kang is a New York native, born and raised just outside New York City. A woman of mixed ethnicities—African American, Native American (Ramapough Lenape Nation), Irish, and Dutch descent—she holds a degree in English with an emphasis on creative writing and a minor in Bible and Christian ministry. She is founder of The Fallow House, and her writing has been featured in *Christianity Today*, *Ekstasis* magazine, She Reads Truth, and (in)courage. Rachel is the author of *Let There Be Art: The Pleasure and Purpose of Unleashing the Creativity within You* and *The Matter of Little Losses: Finding Grace to Grieve the Big (and Small) Things*. Connect with her at rachelmariekang.com and on social media @rachelmariekang.

Dorina Lazo Gilmore-Young is a speaker, podcaster, spoken-word artist, and author of more than twenty books. As a remarried widow, Dorina helps people chase after God's glory on life's unexpected trails and flourish in their God-given callings. Dorina pours her passion into writing books for kids of all ages, teaching the Bible, and coaching high school students in writing. Dorina and her husband, Shawn, are raising three brave daughters in Central California. Together they started the Global Glory Chasers. They love to cook, eat, and travel together. Connect with Dorina at DorinaGilmore.com.

Stacy J. Lowe is a writer and sign language interpreter who loves helping others find encouragement and inspiration through the everyday moments of life. She's a longtime volunteer of several ministries, including her church, and can often be spotted out and about, camera in hand, capturing the beauty of God's handiwork. (Sunrises and sunsets are her favorite to shoot!) She lives in Virginia Beach, Virginia, with her adopted fur baby, Maggie Mae. You can connect with Stacy on Instagram @istacy1011.

Meghan Mellinger is just your average thirtysomething single Christian girl fueled by wanderlust, chai lattes, and loud laughter. A higher education professional by day and writer by night, her goal is to share God's truth in real, humorous, and meaningful ways with young adult women. When she's not booking the next trip on her bucket list, you can catch her eating chips and queso with family and friends. Connect with Meghan on Instagram @megswritesthings.

Dr. Joel Muddamalle holds a PhD in theology and serves as the director of theology and research at Proverbs 31 Ministries. He cohosts the *Therapy & Theology* podcast with Lysa TerKeurst and licensed counselor Jim Cress. Joel is a frequent speaker for churches, conferences, and events. He released his first book, *The Hidden Peace: Finding True Security, Strength, and Confidence Through Humility*, in 2024. Based in Charlotte, North Carolina, Joel and his wife enjoy a full house with their four children and two dogs. If he doesn't have a theology book in hand, you can be sure he's coaching one of his kids in a sport or doing his best to keep up his hoops game on the basketball court. Connect with Joel on Instagram at @muddamalle.

Dr. Avril Occilien-Similien, known as Dr. Avril O, is passionate about walking alongside women as they allow God's truth to transform their hearts and actions. Through her ministry, Flow to Power, she provides tools and resources to encourage, equip, and elevate women in their faith walk. A wife, mother, certified Christian life coach, speaker, author, and executive coach, Dr. Avril O holds a doctorate in leadership and organizational learning, using her expertise to advance God's kingdom both inside and outside the church. She enjoys coffee chats, tea with friends, traveling, and savoring life. To connect with her, visit flowtopower.com.

Brenda Bradford Ottinger believes in authenticity, laughter, hope, prayer, and front porches. She loves her Lord, loves her people, and loves helping others grow rooted in the sacred. The beach is her happy place, and gratitude is worship to her soul. Family, friends, reading, health, and photography are her delights. Brenda is a contributing writer for Proverbs 31 Ministries and lives in North Carolina with her husband and their three sons, who grew up overnight. You can connect with Brenda at BrendaBradfordOttinger.com.

Rachel Booth Smith has a contagious love for God's Word. Her passion to teach accessible theology has led her to develop curriculum, write Bible studies, and teach. She has a master of divinity degree from Pillar Seminary, where she learned to study the Bible in its original languages while being trained in context for the Old Testament and New Testament. Her book, *Rest Assured: What the Creation Story Was Intended to Reveal About Trusting God*, was her passion project. Rachel and her husband have three kids and live in Austin, Texas. You can find more of her writing at rachelboothsmith.com.

Elizabeth Laing Thompson is a speaker and novelist and the author of many inspirational books for women and teens, including *All the Feels: Discover Why Emotions Are (Mostly) Awesome and How to Untangle Them When They're Not*, *All the Feels for Teens: The Good, the Not-So-Good, and the Utterly Confusing*, *When a Friendship Falls Apart: Finding God's Path for Healing, Forgiveness, and (Maybe) Help Letting Go*, and the *When God Says* series. She writes at ElizabethLaingThompson.com about clinging to Christ through the chaos of daily life. Elizabeth believes there is humor in holiness, there is hope in heartache, and coffee goes with everything. She lives in North Carolina with her preacher husband and four kids.

Hadassah Treu is the award-winning international author of *Draw Near: How Painful Experiences Become the Birthplace of Blessings*, a poet, a speaker, and a motivator living in Bulgaria. She is a contributing author to several faith-based platforms like the Koinonia app and Devotable and more than twelve devotional and poetry anthologies. She has been featured on The Upper Room, (in)courage, Proverbs 31 Ministries, Today's Christian Living, Living by Design Ministries, and many other popular sites and podcasts. Connect with Hadassah at onthewaybg.com.

Carrie Zeilstra is the founder of Choosing Faith 23. Through this expanding ministry, Carrie hopes to encourage hurting souls to take refuge in the loving arms of God. She is a member of COMPEL Pro training through Proverbs 31 Ministries and the author of the devotional book *When the Mountain Doesn't Move: 5 Weeks of Choosing Faith*. Carrie lives near Grand Rapids, Michigan, with her husband, son, and cockapoo named Lucy. In addition to writing, she loves coaching gymnastics, teaching at a local university, and hanging out at Lake Michigan beaches. Connect with Carrie at ChoosingFaith23.com.

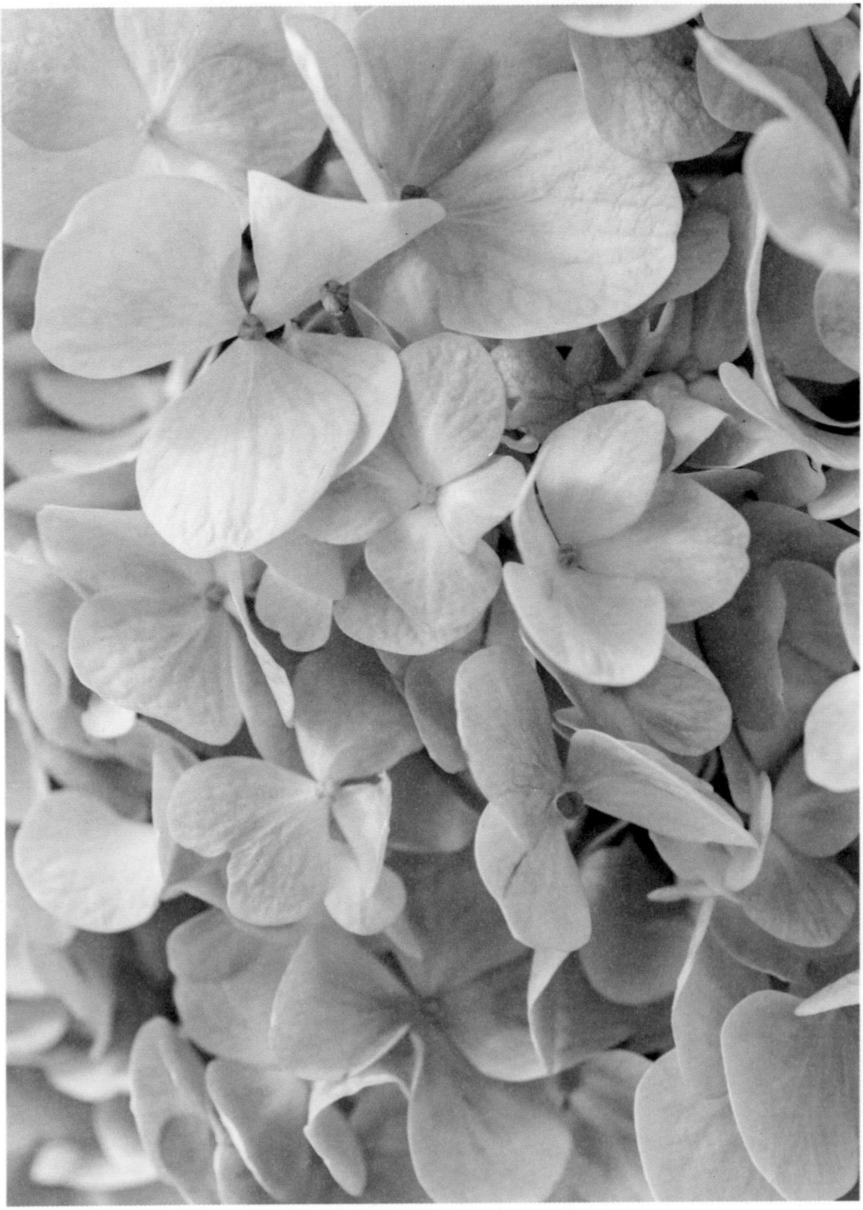

About Proverbs 31 Ministries

Lysa TerKeurst Adams is president and chief visionary officer of Proverbs 31 Ministries.

Proverbs 31 Ministries exists to be a trusted friend who will take you by the hand and walk by your side, leading you one step closer to the heart of God through:

> Free *First 5* Bible study app
> Free online daily devotions
> Circle 31 Book Club
> *The Proverbs 31 Ministries Podcast*
> *Therapy and Theology Podcast*
> COMPEL Pro Writers Training
> She Speaks Conference
> Books and resources

Our desire is to help you to know the Truth and live the Truth. Because when you do, it changes everything.

For more information about Proverbs 31 Ministries, visit www.Proverbs31.org